Introduction

Welcome to the Country Kitchen Wild Food Year book, the first of its kind dedicated to the vast larder which is the British countryside.

The aim of this book is to give you easy to understand guidelines for gathering and enjoying the very best nature has to offer, with plenty of tips about such topics as hunting rabbits, picking blackberries, fishing, gathering wild mushrooms, picking edible flowers and herbs as well as hundreds of recipes and techniques to help you on your way.

Above all, this book is not a survival guide. The idea is not to give up shopping, but to simply enjoy the best of what is out there. For this reason we have condensed the year into three seasons. Wild food from the winter is not at its best, and is much better taken in spring or autumn and left to its own devices in the harshest of months.

One of the thrills of wild food gathering is knowing that your food is fresh, it has not clocked up thousands of air miles, it has not become sad and wilted by the packing, transportation and shelving process, and is just about as good for you as any food could be.

But there is much more to it than even that. I recently picked wild strawberries from a local hillside, and compared them to ones brought from South America and sold in a supermarket. Firstly, the wild ones did not release ten times their own weight of greenhouse gasses into the atmosphere, just to get them into the country. Secondly, in order to get the wild ones, my heart became a little bit healthier because I had to climb the hill in the first place, and thirdly, the wild strawberries grew in a beautiful spot, the view of the surrounding countryside was much nicer than even the very best supermarket shelves.

In my opinion, food from your local countryside cannot be beaten and which ever way you look at it, wild food is good for you, so get out there and enjoy it!

Happy gathering!

Paul Peacock

We would like to thank the following for thier contribution to this book: Heather Acher, Sue Clapham, Dave Costar, Rachel Graham, Lindsay Harriss, Vanessa Kendall, Peter Litfoot, Paul Peacock, Clarissa Porter, Wendy Riddell, Joyce Parker-Sarioglu, Anouchka Warren, and Lucy Young

Published by

KELSEY PUBLISHING LTD

Printed by William Gibbons Ltd.
on behalf of
Kelsey Publishing Ltd, Cudham Tithe Barn, Berry's Hill, Cudham, Kent TN16 3AG
Tel: 01959 541444   *Fax:* 01959 541400
E-mail: kelseybooks@kelsey.co.uk
Website: www.kelsey.co.uk

© 2006
ISBN: 1873098847

THE WILD FOOD YEAR BOOK

Contents

Rules & precautions

Wild food is not free food. There is always a cost associated with collecting food from the wild, and although this is not monetary, it is just as vital. It is important that what we take from the wild is treated with respect, and that we do not fall into the trap of taking indiscriminately.

What we borrow from nature has to be put back, if not by us, by the ecosystems we took from, so practise frugality and use everything to its fullest possible extent. Don't be wasteful and share what you cannot use, recycling what is left.

Do not take more than you need

If you take everything, all the fish, all the rabbits, all the wild garlic, there will be none for next season, and you will only waste the excess anyway. If you take only what you actually need, then the numbers will naturally recover and wild food will remain plentiful.

Keep the spade at home

It is illegal to dig up or uproot any British wild plant; this includes both the rare and the common ones. You are only allowed to uproot any plant, including weeds, with a special licence from the local authority. This, of course, means that wild roots are off the menu.

Preserve!

Preserving wild fruits and plants of all kinds in beers, wines and ciders; salting wild vegetables and fish, smoking meats and making preserved sausages are all ways of extending the way we use and enjoy wild food.

Only collect the best

Leave the mouldy, the moth eaten, the browned and bruised and collect only the very best. But take only what you need.

Don't take our word for it

Just because I can eat one food it doesn't mean you can do the same. With all our advice you have to be careful that you are not going to react badly to a new food. If you decide to experiment and take food not mentioned in this book then make sure you know what you are eating is safe, and only consume a tiny amount at the first sitting.

Experts

If you fancy your chances at country sports, make sure you do it with qualified instructors for your own safety and for the wellbeing of any prey you try for. Never be blasé in the countryside; an enjoyable day's netting rabbits or fishing or shooting will be all the better for a professional attitude.

Environment

Be sure of the purity of the environment from which you take your food. A pigeon found dead under a railway bridge in the city, near a chemical works and a polluted canal will not be safe to eat. If in doubt at all, don't eat.

Spring

Crabbing

Shrimping

Lobster

Dandelion Leaves

Nettles

Herbal Teas

Seashore Vegetables

Edible Weeds

Spring Mushrooms

Edible Flowers

Collecting edible crabs and shrimps

Please be safe on the shore. Beaches are dangerous places, and the world's largest producer of cockles is also the most deadly. Make sure you are safe.

Almost everyone has loaded a crab line with pieces of bacon and pulled out a prickly little green beast, no more than a few inches across and holding on for dear life with one of its claws, only to see it skittle across the sand and back into the sea.

There are two crabs found on our shores which are worth collecting for food, all the rest are either too small or too full of toxins because they prefer to eat near waste pipes. The edible crab is usually as big as a small dinner plate and has a red sandy body with black tips to the claws, and the spider crab looks pretty much like a giant crusty spider.

Edible crabs are usually collected by putting a little bait in a netted box into which the crab can climb, but cannot escape. The traps are quite cheap to buy and if you have a boat to drop them on the sea bed in around twenty feet of water, you should be able to catch a crab a day for your dinner.

You can hunt both edible and spider crabs at low tide by lifting stones near the shoreline. They will not resist being collected, and are quite safe to pick up from the back. Spider crabs congregate in large numbers at low tide in the winter in the southern counties of England, and the long legs are packed with good meat.

All crustaceans should, wherever possible, should be humanly killed. This is best done by placing them in the freezer for at least two hours. They can then be plunged into boiling water where they will feel no pain and death will be instant.

Shrimping can still be done on all our shores where pollution levels are within safe bounds. The basic tool is a push net, so called because you push it along. It is wide and sturdy in the shape of a 'D'. The net is pushed along the floor of the sea at a depth of a foot or so and after a short while enough shrimps for a mouthful are easily collected; an afternoon's work should provide for enough shrimps to make a curry. But you also catch other marine creatures from shore crabs to small fish.

If you go a little further out and sweep the beach with the water at waist height you may be lucky enough to to collect Dover sole and sand eel. The eel can be thrown back, but the Dover sole should be killed and eaten – poached with a slice of lemon.

Push nets are available from Intrex Trading, Darwen, 01254 703516.

There are few better seashore picnics than freshly boiled shrimps. Use a large pan of boiling seawater and toss the shrimps in so they are killed outright. Peel and eat! Fantastic. ●

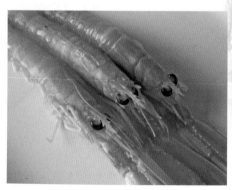

The best in the world!

Britain can make that claim when it comes to shellfish as *Paul Peacock* explains

It is an amazing fact of nature that cold water supports more life than warm, and considering that we in the UK live not that far from the Arctic, we are blessed with the best shellfish in the world.

Our prawns, crabs and lobsters are quite fantastic but sadly the knowledge of how to cook them, simply and for a family, is fast disappearing. Dublin Bay prawn and dressed crab is frequently seen these days as special, but at one time they were commonplace additions to even the poorest tables in the land. Our lobsters are the envy of the world, as are our shore crabs, but sadly because of market forces, these fish are sold for better prices abroad than we are prepared to pay in the UK.

Celebrity chefs are beginning to shout the mantra that has been the unwritten law of

Country kitchen; simplicity! There are hundreds of new cook books on this subject, and it really is the way to cook seafood; simple, bringing out all the flavours of the sea. To achieve a special flavour with seafood takes a little effort and maybe a dip into a perhaps largely forgotten, old fashioned ethos about food.

Whichever way you look at it, food represents valuable nutrition for humans, to be respected as well as enjoyed. Given that the lobster has lost its life to feed us, would it not be something of a pity if we didn't use all of it instead of throwing away the waste? An absolute must, the production of fish stock with the shells and heads, all the bits we don't actually eat, will not only guarantee the fullest use of the food, but will enhance its flavour no end. ●

An absolute must for that taste of the sea.

Fish stock

Boiling, salted water
Fish off-cuts, heads, shells, tails, bones
Rind of ½ lemon
A finely chopped onion
Washing up liquid!

METHOD
Set a large pan of water to boiling and add a teaspoon of salt and the onion.

Wash the fish with cold water and roughly cut up if too large. (Don't use a full crab shell etc)

Carefully add the fish pieces and simmer. Cook for at least an hour and a half. Carefully strain the solid material making sure you leave nothing but liquid.

Set aside to cool naturally in a jar or permanent container. It will most likely set to a jelly overnight, and will freeze as necessary but will not last much longer than a few weeks.

Place your fish pieces in newspaper and cover with washing up liquid; this is the only way I have been able to keep the cats from raiding my dustbin!

Crab

The edible crab is number eight in the BBC's top 50 things you must eat before you die. Every bit as wonderful as lobster, crabs provide a huge amount of meat, and have long been enjoyed within these shores. In the UK crabs are usually sold ready–cooked, and sometimes dressed. Sunday summer salads with dressed crab, cold meats and hard-boiled eggs, soft brown home-made bread and the biggest glass of raspberryade remain one of my longest lasting memories of a complete feast.

Fresh crab

How to dress a crab

Place a cooked crab on its back and remove the claws and legs.

Crack open the claws with a hammer, nut cracker or crab tool, and scoop out the white meat into a bowl.

Do the same for the legs if they are thick enough, but make sure you do not incorporate shell in the meat.

Firmly remove the underside of the crab.

Remove the stomach, which is near the head, the gills and the intestines, leaving only brown meat.

Collect all the brown meat into a second bowl.

Use a toffee hammer to make the shell opening wider and scrub inside and out under running water.

With a fork, lightly mash the white meat adding a little salt and pepper to taste and lemon juice.

You can fill out the brown meat by adding a tablespoon of fine bread-crumbs and season as above. Add a teaspoon of mayonnaise if you want.

Line the shell with lettuce and arrange the two meats in any pattern you like before serving.

You can garnish the sides with parsley.

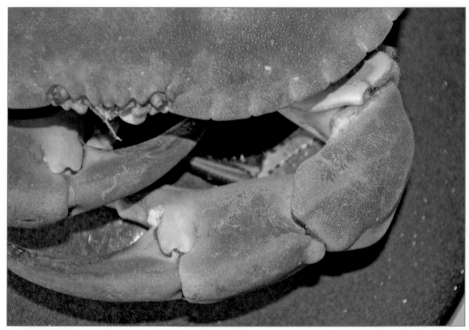

Cooked crab

Crab cakes

You can make this dish with bread-crumbs but potato is more successful. This recipe makes eight crab cakes.

500g (1lb) white crab meat
300g (10oz) mashed potato
A small onion, chopped very finely
Salt and pepper to taste
25g (1oz) parsley

METHOD
Simply combine all the ingredients in a large bowl.

Use a tablespoon to divide into eight portions.

You can coat the cakes in beaten egg for a golden finish. Allow the cakes to stand for a couple of hours, after which they should not fall to pieces in the pan.

Shallow fry each cake in a little oil until golden brown on both sides.

Dressed crab

Lobster

Lobsters are usually sold live in the UK. They will live for a week in the fridge, but should not be kept this long. The RSPCA says that the best way to kill a lobster is to place it into a plastic bag and put it into the deep freeze for at least two hours, where the animal will lose consciousness. It should then be placed straight into boiling water to be cooked. Lobsters should be boiled in a large pan of salted water for 15 minutes plus five minutes for every half kilo.

Live lobster

Lobster bake

As a starter use a lobster for two people, this simple dish is the traditional way to eat this wonderful fish.

1 boiled lobster
150g (5oz) bread-crumbs
1 beaten egg
150g (5oz) cheddar cheese, grated

METHOD
Boil the lobster as above and remove the claws. Break into the claws as for crab and collect the meat.

Cut the animal lengthways into two halves. Discard the gills and the intestines. You can keep the greenish liver and any eggs (known as coral) if the animal was female.

Remove the rest of the meat from the inside of the lobster and mix all the ingredients, except the grated cheese, in a bowl. Carefully wash and scrub out the lobster halves and then fill them with the mixture.

Place on a baking tray and cover with the cheese. Bake for 15 mins at 175°C 350°F/gas 4.

Stuff the lobster with meat, sprinkle with cheese and bake in the oven

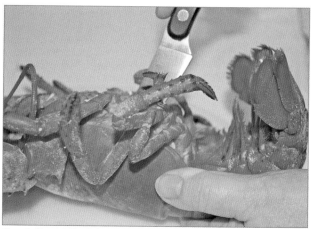

Carefully cut the lobster in half

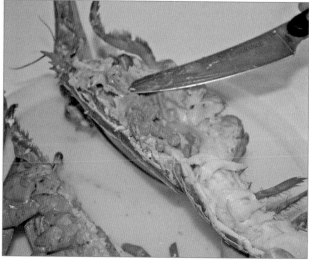

Remove the glassy stomach and roe

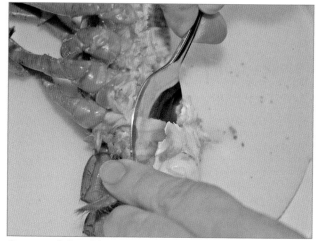

Remove all the white meat and collect

Crack open the claw and remove the meat

Dublin Bay prawn

These are really baby lobsters from Norway, the adults mate to release billions of fry into the Atlantic every year. They follow currents into the nutrient–rich Arctic and wander down the Irish Sea. At one time they were given away as a side catch to white fish. They are eaten as langoustines in France.

Buy them fresh, on ice, and cook them the same day. Remove the head with a knife and pull back on the tail to reveal the flesh, which should simply fall away if you pull on the rings one after the other. Tease away the black gut parts and wash in running water.

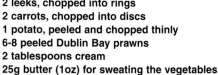

Uncooked Dublin Bay prawn

Dublin Bay prawn soup

This is a great dish, really simple and quite the equal of Bouillabaisse.

1 litre (2 pints) fish stock
2 glasses of white wine
2 leeks, chopped into rings
2 carrots, chopped into discs
1 potato, peeled and chopped thinly
6-8 peeled Dublin Bay prawns
2 tablespoons cream
25g butter (1oz) for sweating the vegetables
Parsley garnish

METHOD

Sweat (steam/fry) the vegetables in butter and a tablespoon of water in a large pan for a few minutes, keeping the lid in place except for stirring. Add the wine and fish stock and bring to the boil. Once boiling, reduce the heat to a simmer. After three or so minutes add the peeled prawns and cook for a further three minutes, no more. You can add other fish if you like, crab meat, white fish, anything. Gently stir in the cream, leaving a little for serving. Stir in a whirl of cream for presentation and serve with a garnish of parsley. Wonderful to eonjoy with freshly baked bread.

Ease the knife under the shell to open the first couple of segments

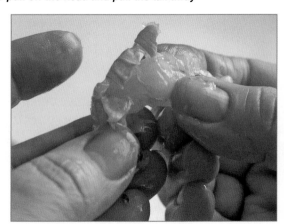

Cut or pull off the head and pull the tail away

Pull the shell away to reveal the flesh

Simply fried with fish sauce

Dublin Bay prawns can be deep fried in oil or steamed for ten minutes and sautéed in butter in a shallow pan. Either way you can serve alone with a slice of lemon or with this delicious fish sauce. This recipe makes a large quantity, but it freezes well.

For the roux:
100g (3½ oz) butter
100g (3½ oz) flour
Pinch of salt
750ml (1½ pints) fish stock
250ml (½ pint) white wine
100ml (4fl oz) single cream
Milk for consistency

METHOD

Combine the wine and the fish stock and simmer to reduce by two thirds Melt the butter in a hot pan and beat in the salted flour to make a roux, working out the lumps. Add the hot liquid and cook over a medium heat, beating all the time. Once thickened, add the cream and stir. Should you not be happy with the consistency, incorporate a little warmed milk. Add extra seasoning as required, crushed black peppercorns are a particularly tasty addition.

Keep the shell for stock making – clean any gut from the flesh

Potted shrimps

This has to be a classic British dish, but I wonder how many of you have tried it. It is so very simple, easy, quick and tasty, but somehow it has almost disappeared. And it's cheap to make, but expensive to buy ready-made, which I always think is a good reason for doing it yourself. That way you can make bigger portions, rather than the mean little pots you sometimes see in shops. Shrimps are the classic ingredient, but you could substitute crab or lobster. So off you go, and make sure you use shrimps, not prawns!

Serves 6

450g (1lb) fresh shrimps
150g (5oz) clarified butter
2 tsp lemon juice, or anchovy essence depending on ingredients
Pinch of mace
Pinch of cayenne pepper to taste
Nutmeg (optional)
Salt

METHOD
Preheat the oven to 180°C, (355°F, gas 4-5). If you bought raw shrimps, boil them for two minutes, but you probably bought cooked shrimps.

Peel the shrimps. Melt half of the butter and add the seasonings (use the anchovy essence with shrimps, and lemon juice with crab or lobster). Put the shrimps in an oven dish and pour over the butter with the seasoning. Bake for 20 minutes.

Remove and strain off the butter, putting it to one side. Pack the shrimps into smaller dishes, such as ramekins. Take the butter you have put aside from the cooking and pour over the shrimps in the pots. Leave them to cool and set.

Melt and clarify the remaining butter, and then pour over the dishes to form a buttery cover about 6mm thick. Try not to get any air trapped beneath the butter.

Chill in a fridge, and serve with crisp lettuce, and thinly sliced toast.

Spider crabs. The long legs are packed full of tasty meat!

Dandelion

The dandelion is named after the shape of its leaves, which look, apparently, like lion's teeth. It is also known as the bitterwort, which should give you some indication of what it tastes like.

It is an enormously nutritious vegetable and should be taken by everyone, and indeed if the Victorians hadn't stopped its cultivation due to changing culinary fashions, there would have been a lot less gout in the world.

The young leaves are best taken as they appear; otherwise they get to be too bitter. They can be blanched, like endives, by placing a flower pot over the dandelion and allowing the bitterness to reduce.

Dandelion leaves are most frequently used as a part of a mixed salad. Cut your dandelion leaves into small pieces and mix them with ten times as much lettuce, rocket, nasturtium and any other leaves you have to hand. This, with a little lemon juice, will make a wonderful green salad.

You can do other things with dandelion leaves. They can be combined with nettles, for example, boiled and blended with a little cream stirred in for a really tasty early spring meal.

The dandelion is an important plant for the so-called hungry gap. This is the time when much of the stored food is all used up and the first crops of the spring have not yet appeared. It is no longer used as such, but its widespread status is down to the fact that everyone grew the plant for just that time of the year.

One last word about dandelion leaves, be careful which ones you pick and wash them thoroughly. They can be a fpopular watering site for cats, so if you collect them in an urban area, be aware. Also, as with many edible 'weeds' you should ensure they have not been sprayed with weed killers or other chemicals.

● *Also known as 'Poor man's saffron' the dandelion florets can be used, wrapped in muslin, to colour dishes from rice to blancmange*

Grasping the nettle

Okay, hands up how many of you have been stung by nettles? Now here's your chance to get your own back on this highly nutritious, yet confrontational, plant

By **Peter Litfoot**

Keeping well covered up when harvesting!

Remember you should wear gloves while washing fresh nettles

The Stinging Nettle (Urtica dioica) comes in 30 different varieties and has had many uses over the centuries. Roman conquerors made tea from it and allegedly used to whip themselves with it to keep themselves warm in the cooler British climate. During World War II, nettles were used to make green camouflage paint, the fibres from nettles have been used to make cloth, and nettles are still used today by gardeners to make a natural fertiliser by simply soaking them in a bucket of water.

Nettles grow almost anywhere, especially in the countryside. They are indeed a very difficult weed to control, invading fields in the same way as docks and thistles. They spread impressively with travelling radial sprouting roots and from around July the wind will blow their seeds far and wide to colonise fresh ground. Unsurprisingly, most animals will not consider eating fresh stinging nettles, which is another reason why it grows so well, although some species of caterpillars thrive on it. As the stinging hairs are only around the edge of the leaf, caterpillars are probably a lot more successful than, say, a cow would be, at managing to have their nettle feast without getting stung. Having said that, people have been known to hold nettle-eating competitions using nasty fresh nettles.

'the sting of the Nettle is but nothing compared to the pains that it heals'

Harvesting

It's best to use the young shoots or the tips (the top 2-3cm) of the nettles, certainly not the tough stem. Just pick the clean tips, you don't want them if they have bird droppings on them – apart from anything else, it doesn't come off that easily! If the top leaves are curled-in on themselves then they are also best avoided as they probably have young caterpillars hatching out on them. Nettles can normally be harvested from late March up to September. If you want to get some young tender shoots later in the season, the best thing to do is to cut the nettles back to the ground and then allow them to grow again. Nettles can be washed and cooked fresh or they can be dried for use when out of season.

Revenge of the nettles

Protect yourself from stings while harvesting the nettles by making sure you are suitably clothed, with a long sleeved top and some good quality gloves. The tiny hairs that sting you have little reservoirs of formic acid at their base which they inject into your skin on contact. Vigorous rubbing of dock leaves over any stings on the skin has been said to help alleviate the pain. This may be true, but it is often suggested that relief here is more psychological than real. Either way it's a good way to make your skin go green! Once dried or cooked the sting is completely removed.

'... be sure to test your experiments before feeding them to your in-laws!'

A magical herb

It has been said that 'the sting of the Nettle is but nothing compared to the pains that it heals.' As well as being highly nutritious, nettles are recommended to help cure a huge list of ailments. We won't guarantee it works, but they've been used for the conditions of alopecia, asthma, dropsy, gout, rheumatism, skin disease, jaundice, gingivitis and tonsillitis. They are also reputed to purify the blood, prevent cramps and even to eliminate body odour (you drink the infusion – don't go rubbing fresh leaves into your armpits!). Numerous products are available on the market made from nettle leaves and roots.

Recipe ideas...

Nettle omelettes

Nettle omelette is very quick and easy to make, and when flavoured with herbs can be very tasty. Preparation and cooking time 12 to 15 minutes.

Nettle tops – washed, one cup full
2 eggs
A little milk
Herbs (oregano, parsley, chives, tarragon)
Seasoning

METHOD

Boil nettle tips for 7 minutes
Whisk up eggs and milk
Add seasonings and herbs
Strain and add nettles
Heat a little oil in a saucepan
Add mixture
Fry for 3 minutes

Nettle soup

For nettle soup you can try using many different herbs and vegetables, but be sure to test your experiments before feeding them to your in-laws! My first attempt at an ad-hoc nettle soup was a complete disaster and it didn't go down at all well with the family. I have since refined the ingredients I use, and, I kid you not, my in-laws' only word to describe the soup from the recipe here, was a unanimous 'delicious'. And it is! Preparation and cooking time 45 minutes.

Serves 4

Three bowls of nettle tops
One bowl of chopped onions
One bowl of chopped carrots
One bowl of chopped parsnips or swede or turnips
2 tbsp flour
3 tbsp cooking oil
3 tbsp butter
500ml (1 pint) stock (chicken or vegetable)
Chopped clove of garlic, or garlic chives
Pepper, salt (optional)
2 sprigs of rosemary, thyme and 2 bay leaves

METHOD

Heat the oil in a large frying pan and cook the onions carrots and parsnips on a medium heat for 10 minutes
Mix in the butter, then add the flour, then the stock, then the stinging nettles, garlic, herbs and seasoning
Mix well, cover the pan and cook on a low heat for 30 minutes
Remove bay leaves then liquidise, the soup can then be re-heated and served or frozen.

Nettle tea

You can make nettle tea either with dried leaves or fresh leaves. Boil 20 grams of dried leaves in a pint of water for three minutes. Alternatively use a cupful of fresh leaves. Strain out the leaves and your nettle tea is ready and very drinkable. If you like, you can sweeten it with honey or unrefined cane sugar. As an alternative, try adding a sprig of rosemary, thyme or lavender before boiling or some lemon juice after boiling.

Nettle haggis

This recipe is a meaty haggis, for a vegetarian version the pork could be replaced with sweet chestnuts. You can also add in your favourite herbs. Preparation time 30 minutes, cooking time one hour.

Serves 4

4 bowls of nettle tops
2 leeks
2 onions
Half a cabbage
500g (1lb) pork mince or quorn
1 bowl of soaked oats
½ bowl of barley
Sage, thyme and salt

METHOD

Fry the leeks, onions and pork in a large pan, medium heat for 10 minutes
Add the nettles, cabbage, herbs and two cups of water, cook for another 10 minutes
Add the barley and mix well, take off the heat and add the oats, again mix well
Roll the mixture into two or three balls, sprinkle on salt and wrap tightly in a muslin cloth, tying both ends
Hang for one or two days, you can then freeze it or boil for an hour to serve.

Nutritionist's view
Louise Sutton

The stinging nettle is well established and highly regarded in the world of herbal medicine. Nettle leaf has become a popular treatment for allergies, such as hayfever and asthma. A preliminary study suggested that freeze-dried nettle leaf taken in supplement form improved allergy symptoms, whilst recent animal studies involving rats have reported that extracts of nettle lowered blood pressure, reduced heart rate and displayed a noticeable diuretic effect.

From a nutritional standpoint, nettles are reportedly high in many essential nutrients. Nettle leaves are a powerhouse of vitamins and minerals, such as vitamins A and C, calcium, iron and copper, and it is due to their nutritional value that nettles have traditionally been given in soups and teas to the anaemic, debilitated and recuperating.

As with other green vegetables, the leaves are also a rich source of flavinoids – phytochemicals thought to play a role in maintaining health, particularly in reducing our risk of heart disease and cancer. In addition they are said to dish up more protein than any other green vegetable.

But before you swap your spinach for a plate full of this nasty weed, a word of caution, ingesting large quantities can cause some undesirable side effects including constipation, stomach ache and skin burning. It should also be noted that nettle products, like many herbs, are not recommended during pregnancy.

Nutritional content

Vitamin A	Potassium
Vitamin C	Silica
Protein	Sulphur
Iron	Iodine
Manganese	beta carotene

Nettle beer

Before hops were used more widely, from the 17th century, ale in England, and elsewhere would have been made from many different plants, including nettles. Nettle beer can still be purchased in some places in the UK (see below). It's very easy to make, if you cannot get lager yeast, you can use baking yeast, check the label on the tin (but don't use bread making yeast). Please also note that cream of tartar is nothing to do with tartar sauce – it's a dry powder normally sold in a small tub alongside baking products. Our nettle beer looked, and even tasted, a little like scrumpy cider. In our tasting trials more than half the people we got to try it liked it but not many felt they could manage a whole pint!

1kg (2lb) nettles
500g (1lb) brown sugar
2 lemons
25g (1oz) cream of tartar
Lager yeast

METHOD

In a large pan, boil nettles in 2 litres (4 pints) of water for half an hour
Strain out the pulp, add and dissolve the sugar, add the juice of the lemons and cream of tartar
Transfer to a gallon jar and top up with water, add the yeast
Fit an air lock and leave for three days, then siphon off from the sediment into another gallon jar before bottling
Leave for three days before you drink it

Nettle wine

If you are interested in making your own wine then you really must try using nettles.

6 bowls of nettle tops
1 bowl of raisins
Approx 1kg (2.2lb) of sugar
Yeast nutrient
Yeast for wine making
2 lemons
2 campden tablets

METHOD

Rinse the nettles and boil in water with one of the lemons
Drain and press out all liquid from the pulp and put into the fermentation container

Dissolve sugar into the liquid and top up to a gallon
When at room temperature add the raisins, yeast nutrient, juice from the second lemon and campden tablets. Mix, cover with sterile cloth and leave to stand for a day
Add the yeast and stir daily for around five days until it stops frothing
Siphon off into demijohn and fit airlock
Once the wine has gone clear, siphon off into another demijohn and re-fit the air lock
After three months the wine should be ready for bottling, however it is best left for a full year before drinking

As an alternative, try adding rosemary, thyme, lavender, ginger or parsley (or any other flavoured herb) instead of the raisins.

Tongue tingling Stinger Ale!

Made from Hugh Fearnley-Whittingstall's own crop of organic nettles in Dorset, Stinger Ale is brewed by Hall & Woodhouse, the company that brews Badger Ales. Stinger is the result of a very enjoyable series of experiments guided by the Hall & Woodhouse Head Brewer, Dr Tim Morris. In his opinion the ale has a grassy herbal aroma with subtle gooseberry and lemon citrus notes that build up towards the end of the glass. It is finished with a slightly spicy aftertaste that lingers beautifully. Now, if that doesn't make you want to try it, what will? While perhaps not having as highly developed taste buds as a head brewer, we think we know what he means! We also have to concede that the ale was a little more drinkable than the one we made! The ale is priced from £1.89 per ½ litre bottle and is available for sale at www.Badgerdirect.com, and at the Hall & Woodhouse Brewery Shop, Blandford St Mary, Dorset, and also at selected Hall & Woodhouse pubs.

" I'm delighted with the results. I think we have a delicious and refreshing beer with character and real depth; properly hoppy with that little tingle of stinger from the nettles. It's good summer drinking, and seems to be slipping down a treat with the barbecued mackerel "

Hugh Fearnley-Whittingstall

Herbal teas

If you are a fan of putting assorted bits of woodland in a cup of boiling water, you will already know about the health giving, calming and restorative nature of herbal tea. But more than just medicine, herbal tea is both fun and flavoursome.

Most culinary herbs have their uses in tea, some refresh, others relax and still more simply taste wonderful. It is said that we all of us drink too much ordinary tea and coffee. Try to replace one cup with a glass of water in the morning and another with an herbal tea in the afternoon. You will reap the benefits within a short time; have a better complexion, will sleep more restfully and your liver and kidneys will have an easier job because there will be fewer toxins in your system to deal with.

Experiment

To make herbal tea, collect the fresh herb and use as soon as possible. Use small quantities to start with, increasing the strength to taste. To help the herbs infuse you can chop them up before you use them. If you need to sweeten, use honey instead of sugar and a slice of lemon makes an ideal accompaniment.

If you are taking herbal teas for medical reasons, it is important you see your doctor, especially if you are taking any medication or you are pregnant, and if your symptoms persist a few days.

HERB	PART USED	BENEFITS	NOTES
Celery	Seeds or leaf	Digestion problems are soothed by this tea	
Chamomile	Flowers and leaves	Tension and tummy ache	Do not suck the raw leaves, they can cause blisters
Dandelion	Young leaves, sometimes bruised root	Urinary difficulties	Seek medical help if you continue to experience problems
Elderflower	Flower heads	Helps with colds and blocked sinus	Shake all the insects out first
Fennel	Seed and leaf	Digestive problems	Aniseed flavour
Lemon balm	Leaf	Soothing relaxant for the anxious	
Marigold	Flower	Anti bacterial	Antiseptic of yesteryear
Mint	Leaf	Wonderful for the digestion	Completely safe
Nettle	Leaf	Detoxification and general pick me up	
Rosemary	Leaf	Antiseptic and pain relief	Can increase blood pressure
Rose petal	Petal	Calming	
Sage	Leaf	Antiseptic and excellent astringent	Do not use in pregnancy

You can make combination teas, rose petal and blackberry leaf, for example, makes a wonderfully flavoured tea, and you can use all kinds of fruit from the garden from blackcurrants to strawberries. Experiment away, but most of all, enjoy!

Sea vegetables

Sandra Geere introduces an unusual food source that we all can enjoy, wherever we live

One of the greatest pleasures of overseas travel is to discover different food and sample the delights of new flavours and textures. What a pity we are not as adventurous with the wild food that grows on and around our own shores. Sea vegetables are a perfect example of food that is largely ignored, yet can be a delicious and highly nutritious addition to our diet.

Sea vegetables include seaweed found in the sea and plants found on rocks and shorelines washed by the tide, and salty mud marshes. Both types contain (in varying quantities) protein, fibre, the antioxidant beta-carotene, iodine (used to treat thyroid problems), potassium, calcium, copper, zinc, manganese and vitamins A, B, B2, B12, C and D.

Laver, a brown seasweed, can be found on rugged, coastlines around the UK, mainly on the western coasts and where it can attach itself to embedded rocks. It's rich in protein, iodine, vitamins and very low in calories. This has made it popular as a health food but it's often presented in the shops in tablet form which seems like such a waste.

Bilberries grow abundantly around beachy areas, mainly further north in Britain. They're small branched shrubs, with wiry angular branches, rarely over a foot high, and the black berries, which are blackcurrant-sized are covered with a grey, misty bloom when ripe. The leaves which are leathery can be used in tea.

Sea kale is unfortunately reclining in Britain because of sea-defence work but can still be found. It grows in large clumps of grey-green leaves with purple stalks, and in summer with clusters of white flowers which smell sweet and attract insects. As with all plants it's best to choose young shoots and leaves, but the stems of Sea Kale in particular can become quite woody.

Samphire contains silica and in the fourteenth century glassmakers located their workshops in areas where the plant grew. Samphire ashes were also used to make soap although you certainly wouldn't make the connection when you eat it! Shakespeare mentions samphire in King Lear and Culpepper, writing in the seventeenth century, advocated its use for digestive problems and flatulence. Pickled samphire was taken on ocean voyages to help sailors combat scurvy.

No known seaweed is poisonous but concerns have sometimes been raised about sea pollution and its effect on food safety. In July 2004 the Food Standards Agency reported that tests carried out on a number of seaweeds revealed high levels of arsenic in Japanese Hijiki. Eaten regularly it can increase people's risk of developing cancer. Hijiki is the very dark, shredded seaweed sometimes used in

Samphire

(Basic preparation)

For each person allow a small handful of young samphire shoots. Wash thoroughly in cold water and remove any tough pieces of stem. Place in a large saucepan of boiling water for two to three minutes or just enough time to blanch them but retain a 'crunch'. Drain well and place in a serving dish. Traditionally samphire was served with melted butter and vinegar but I prefer lemon juice and freshly ground black pepper. Serve with any baked or grilled fish and new potatoes.

Pickled samphire

1 colanderful washed samphire with tough stems removed
1½ pints (855ml) white vinegar
½ pint (285ml) water
1 teaspoon salt
3 teaspoons pickling spice
1 teaspoon ground mace
6 peppercorns

METHOD

Soak samphire in salted water for one hour. Rinse in cold water and drain. Put in a large saucepan with enough cold water to cover, bring to the boil, cook for ten minutes and drain well. Boil the vinegar, water, salt and spices together for five minutes, then leave to cool. Fill sterilised jars with samphire to within ½ inch of the top. Strain the spiced vinegar into a jug and pour over the samphire and seal the jars with vinegar-proof lids. Store for three months before using. Pickled samphire is delicious with cold meats and fish.

Japanese restaurants but not in sushi or in Chinese restaurants. The Food Standards Agency claims that occasional consumption is unlikely to significantly raise the risk of developing cancer. However, consumers should check ingredients in foods eaten by vegetarians and vegans.

The salt content of seaweed can be high. But thorough washing and salt-free cooking will overcome this. Seaweed can also be included in the diet in the form of kelp tablets.

For devotees of fast food burgers research undertaken at Newcastle University appears to offer a compromise. Apparently, by removing some of the fat from, for example pies, burgers and cakes and replacing it with seaweed extract, it is possible to improve their quality by adding fibre and improving the flavour, allegedly making them healthier.

Japanese seaweeds are sold in strips in health stores, speciality shops and a few larger supermarkets either dried or in vacuum packs. They can be chopped, shredded or crumbled for use in soups, salads, meat and fish dishes or with rice.

Most seaweeds can be harvested between May and September but the best months to gather them are May and June when the plants are young and tender. Before cooking, wash all seaweed carefully in plenty of fresh water.

Although found all around Britain's coastline, laver is most popular and widely available in

Wales where it is gathered when the tide has gone out. Low in calories and rich in minerals it is translucent, thin and wavy-edged. To make laverbread first cook the laver to a purée, shape into cakes by coating in oatmeal and fry. Laverbread is traditionally served with bacon and tomatoes.

Sea beet (sea spinach) grows like cultivated spinach on coastal paths and sea walls and can be harvested from June to October. It is especially rich in beta-carotene and used in the same way as garden spinach.

Of all the sea vegetables my favourite is samphire for its fleshy stems, bright green colour and fresh taste. It grows on the tide mostly in Norfolk and Suffolk (also Brittany) between May and August. I buy samphire from the fishmonger at my local market and start pestering him for it on the first of May! You are unlikely to find it in the supermarket so ask your fishmonger to source a supply for you.

The sea has so much more to offer than fish, delicious as it is. Perhaps, as part of our sustainability strategy, it is time for us as consumers to explore what else our coasts have to offer and to start demanding a little more imagination from our shops and supermarkets. ●

Norfolk crab and samphire soup

1 dressed crab
1 medium potato
500g (1lb) cleaned samphire
600ml (1 pt) stock (meat or light vegetable)
50g (2oz) butter
200ml (8floz) single cream
Freshly ground black pepper

METHOD
Peel and finely slice the potato and sauté slowly in butter in a closed saucepan until soft. Boil the samphire for 5-15 minutes and slide all the green flesh off the stalks. Add the samphire to the potatoes and continue to sauté for a couple of minutes adding the stock. Bring to the boil then liquidise until smooth. Return the liquid to the pan and stir in the crab meat. Add the cream and pepper to taste. Bring to simmering point only and remove from the heat. Serve hot or chilled.

Where to buy: Healthfood and speciality shops, larger supermarkets and fishmongers. For a real treat visit Cookie's Crab Shop and restaurant in Salthouse, North Norfolk for fresh samphire, also pickled samphire at £3.50 for a large jar. Contact Peter and Suzanne McKnespiey on 01263 740352 for opening times.

Mushrooms

Although mushrooms are often most readily associated with Autumn and its 'mellow fruitfulness', some species are true heralds of Spring. **Sue Clapham** introduces the Morel and the St George's mushroom

Morels (Morchella spp) seem to inspire more lyrical writing and flights of fancy than any other species of fungi. One expert describes them as "shrouded in mystery, inflaming human passions and able to cloak themselves in invisibility". Another speaks of them having a peculiar sense of humour, while a third tells the, possibly apocryphal, tale of an elderly European lady who "on her deathbed, called her niece home from America so that she could whisper in her ear the location of her private Morel haunt."

There are descriptions of "Morelmania" taking hold in parts of America, where competitions are held to see who can gather the most in a given time, the hunters being helped by regular updates in the local media as to the whereabouts and condition of that year`s crop and this activity taking precedence over everything else during the Morels' short fruiting season.

Much of the mystique surrounding Morels seems to stem from their habit of popping up in strange and unpredictable places and nearly always well camouflaged. For some it is more the fun of the chase than the actual eating which captures the imagination.

Morels start to fruit after the first warm rains, just as the trees are coming into leaf. They thrive, between April and June, in abandoned apple orchards, at the foot of dying and dead elms, around oaks and poplars or in the sandy, gravelly soil associated with rivers, streams or even sewage works.

They are also renowned for their ability to come to life after a serious fire, such as hit the Yellowstone National Park in America in 1988, or even a devastating volcano such as the Mount St. Helen`s eruption, after which some of the largest Morel finds in history were discovered emerging from the volcanic ash.

That said though, Morels are not necessarily dependent on any of these conditions and have been discovered in pots of chrysanthemums, after a flood which left a family`s backyard under a foot of water for more than a week and in the ashes of an indoor fireplace which had not been used for six months.

Colourful treats

Of the varieties most prized for their flavour, the Black Morel (variously Morchella angusticeps, M conica and M. elata) tends to appear first, with its typical deeply ribbed cap and white, hollow stem. Described as "robust and flavourful" it can reach four to six inches in length.

The Yellow Morel (Morchella esculenta) which puts in a slightly later appearance, is said to be the tastiest and most sought after. Despite its common name, Morchella esculenta ranges in colour from light grey to dark grey, light tan to golden yellow, yellow to dark brown. The shape of the cap can vary from long and pointed to short and squat but must still have that "honeycombed" appearance.

(For False Morels note the Warning below)
Enthusiasts claim that Morels rank just below Perigord truffles in taste and "for those who have eaten enough of both fungi to develop a palate, there is serious debate about which is tastiest."

There is little debate about how they should be handled however. Cut the fruit rather than pulling it up as rough treatment can damage the sub-terranean mycelium, the actual mushroom organism, thereby reducing future harvests.

And if the idea of hunting Morels doesn't appeal?

Until relatively recently it was impossible to grow your own Morels and even though the spawn for Morchella angusticeps is now available from speciality suppliers, cultivation is still a hit and miss affair.

Ann Miller, who has been developing an appropriate strain for the UK for several years, says there are no guarantees but suggests two possible approaches.

The spawn, supplied on grain, can be mixed up to four inches deep into the ash and charred wood of an old bonfire site, provided no plastic or other inorganic rubbish has been burnt there and it is in a shaded site. Water the site well (autumn may be the optimum time for this as there is less chance of the spawn drying out) and then leave it until April when it should again be watered if there is no rain.

If there is no suitable site available it is possible to make up a mixture which will simulate a suitable growing environment.

"Try mixing one part spawn to 10 parts peat, five parts wood ash and one part gypsym," Ann suggests. "In a shaded area, clear the topsoil to a depth of four inches. Mix all the ingredients well, fill the site and then treat it in the same way as before. With luck Morels will develop in May or June but it can take two years before they appear."

The delicate and fragile flesh is described as being "woodsy and nutlike", with a "strong aromatic flavour and a characteristically spicy fragrance". Morels must be cooked and, as with so many fungi, the simplest treatment – sautéed in butter until lightly browned – enhances their flavour the best.

Alternatively, they can be sautéed in olive oil, garlic and a little Marsala wine or soaked in milk, coated in a half-and-half mixture of flour and cornflour and then fried in hot olive oil with garlic or shallots.

They make a good soup and go well with pasta but for a real marriage made in heaven try Morels with fresh spring asparagus – sautéed in butter and garlic and served with a squeeze of lemon juice and freshly ground black pepper.

Romantic roots

Any article on Spring mushrooms should include a mention of The St. George`s Mushroom (Calocybe gambosum) which, despite romantic stories about the Saint presenting some to the Hungarians who thence named it after him, is probably more mundanely named because of its appearance around the 23rd April.

Whatever the case, the sight of the bright white fruiting bodies appearing in succulent young grass, often in the form of a "fairy ring", is very welcome when so much else is in short supply.

Preferring hedgerows, fields and grassy woodlands, Calocybe gambosum has white gills which are notably narrow and crowded together. Its compact flesh has a distinctive floury or "mealy" smell and makes a good stroganoff when other mushrooms may not be readily available, or similarly can be used in a savoury soufflé.

So whether it be the Morel, that enigmatic prima donna of the fungi world, or the easily-spotted St. George`s, there is no excuse for missing out on a good mushroom feast in the Spring.

WARNING: Morels are quite distinctive but there is a small chance they could be confused with False Morels (helvella & gyromitra spp) which can be fatal at worst or induce extremely unpleasant symptoms. Always take advice from an expert if in any doubt at all., including mushrooms grown in the garden.

Allergies: Some people are allergic to mushrooms and mushroom spores or can become sensitised to high concentrations of spores.

Cleaning Morels: Morels do need cleaning because they can harbour grit and insects etc but be as sparing as possible when washing them and allow to dry before use.

Cooking: Morels must be cooked as they can irritate the stomach if eaten raw.

Tony Heath`s Warm Salad of St. George`s mushrooms, broad beans, pine kernels with organic herb leaves & tarragon dressing

200g (8oz) St. George`s Mushrooms
1 handful broad beans, shelled
½ shallot, finely chopped
½ clove garlic, finely chopped
½ tbsp olive oil
½ tbsp pine kernels, lightly toasted
1 bag mixed salad leaves
½ tbsp freshly chopped flat leaf parsley
Sea salt & freshly ground black pepper

METHOD

Blanch the beans and rinse in cold water to prevent discolouring. Cut the mushrooms into an even size, the smaller ones can be left whole. Heat a non-stick pan and add the olive oil. Add the shallots and garlic followed by the mushrooms. Constantly stir or toss the mixture for 2-3 minutes until the mushrooms slightly colour. Add the broad beans, season with sea salt & pepper.

Tarragon Dressing

2 shallots, chopped
1 clove garlic, chopped
150ml (5fl oz) red wine
150ml (5fl oz) red wine vinegar
1 tsp Dijon Mustard
300ml (10fl oz) olive oil
Seasoning
Snipped tarragon leaves

METHOD

Place the chopped shallots and garlic in a pan with the red wine and reduce until almost dry. Add the vinegar and reduce by three-quarters. Remove from the heat and stir in the Dijon mustard and blend in the olive oil. Season and add a few chopped tarragon leaves. Cover, cool and bottle. The dressing will keep for a few weeks.

To Serve

Spoon the mushroom mixture onto a plate and carefully place a small pile of salad leaves on top of the mushrooms. Drizzle a little tarragon dressing over the salad and sprinkle with toasted pine kernels and chopped parsley.

Stuffed Morels

1 dozen medium sized Morels
250g (9oz) flaked crabmeat
1 egg, beaten
120ml (4fl oz) oil
2 tbsp mayonnaise
2 tbsp finely chopped onion
2 tsp lemon juice
50g (2oz) seasoned breadcrumbs
2 tbsp melted butter

METHOD

In a bowl combine the crabmeat, egg, oil, mayonnaise, onion, lemon juice and half the breadcrumbs Fill the Morels with the mixture and place in an ovenproof dish. Combine the remaining breadcrumbs with melted butter and sprinkle over. Bake at 190°C (375°, gas 5) for approximately 15 minutes.

References & Suppliers:

Morel recipes reproduced with kind permission of Brad Wildermuth of www.thegreatmorel.com/index.shtml, a fund of stories, pictures and recipes.
St. George`s Mushroom recipe by kind permission of Tony Heath at Let`s Eat www.letseatperth.co.uk

Ann Miller`s Speciality Mushrooms Ltd: all you need for growing a wide range of edible mushrooms in your garden. Green Bank, Meikle Wartle, Inverurie, Aberdeenshire AB51 5AA Tel/Fax 01467 671 315, email: ann@annforfungi.co.uk

Mycologue: A mushroom collector`s catalogue, selling everything from knives to baskets to Fungi Holidays in France. Tel 02074857063, email: mycologue@lewy.force9.net

The Mycologist: The international journal of general Mycology, Quarterly. The British Mycological Society, PO Box 30, Stourbridge, West Midlands DY9 9PZ. Tel 01562 887043

Journal of the Association of British Fungus Groups, Quarterly, for those interested in all aspects of fungi. Michael Jordan, Chantry House, Channards Grave, Somerset BA44 4LY Tel 01749 346967. email: ABFG@chantryhouse.demon.co.uk

Books:
Mushrooms and other Fungi of Great Britain Roger Phillips (1994). An excellent book for identification, comprehensive and beautifully illustrated.
Mushrooms in the Garden Helllmut Steineck (1993). For the amateur gardener growing exotic mushrooms for their own consumption.
Growing Gourmet and Medicinal Mushrooms Paul Stamets (1993).Basic microbiological techniques for the serious grower including temperature, humidity and substrate requirements for a range of speciality mushrooms.
In The Company of Mushrooms Elio Schaechter (1998). A delightful and informative account of the mysterious life of fungi.

Sautéed Morels with cream

15–20 Morels, cut in half if large
1 large shallot, finely chopped
1 large clove garlic, finely chopped
2 tbsp unsalted butter
2 tbsp olive oil
120ml (4fl oz) chicken stock
240ml (8fl oz) cream

METHOD

Put the olive oil in a heated pan over a medium heat. Stir in the garlic and shallot and sauté until softened but not browned. Add butter and, when it has melted, add Morels. Stir & cook until the mushrooms start to brown – about four minutes. Add stock and cook for a further 2-3 minutes. Add cream and cook on low until reduced and thickened.
Classically served on toast, but brilliant on grilled steaks.

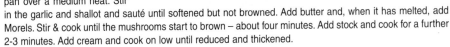

Hedgerow weeds

The textbook definition of a weed is a plant growing in the wrong place. But who said it was the wrong place? The weed? So many of what we would call weeds today have been priceless plants in the past, gathered together for all sorts of reasons, some culinary, some aesthetic, some medical. On the whole their important past has been forgotten and a multi billion pound industry has sprung up in trying to get rid of them.

Words of warning

If you have any medical complaint at all, do not pick and consume wild plants. This is important because some plants interfere with drugs, others can cause unpleasant and severe allergic reactions which make certain medical conditions worse and some can sometimes cause problems in pregnancy.

A little botany

Plants with flowers arranged like umbrellas are related to the carrot and parsnip, and are called, unsurprisingly, the Umbelliferae. Apart from one or two well known examples such as hemlock, this group of plants are all edible.

If you are worried about allergy problems with a member of this group, then the more it smells like a strongly smelling parsnip, the more likely the chances are for allergy problems. If in doubt, don't eat. The plants that have yellow or white flowers with four petals in the shape of a cross are called the Cruciferae and are all pretty much safe to eat.

Plants that have flowers which look like a number of tiny flowers, almost dandelion like, have composite flower heads and are therefore grouped into the Compositae. Most of these plants are safe to eat.

Make sure you do not collect plants of any kind from any place where they might have been sprayed or contaminated by pollution. Industrial, inner city, watercourses are packed with edible plants, but these specimens are most likely to have high concentrations of heavy metals, dioxins, toxins from sewage plants and can even contain high concentrations of human hormones, particularly oestrogens. If in doubt, don't pick.

Not all the wild plants out there are safe to eat, so be careful, but don't let any thoughts of being poisoned to death put you off! In the next few pages you will find dozens of species that you can make an excellent meal of and our special favopurites from the magazine are there in more detail.

Wild Garlic

You are walking past a damp hillside when suddenly you are overtaken by the smell of garlic. Growing in the damp soil you find a little plant that looks something like a lilly with little spiky white flowers. This is wild garlic, or Ransomes as it is often referred to.

You can use this plant just like garlic, except you use it all; roots, bulb, leaves, stem and flower. Simply chop it up and add to stews or even use it in salads. The very best omelette in the world is made from chopped Ransomes and fried for a few seconds just before the beaten egg is thrown in.

Hogweed (Heracleum sphodylium)

Hogweed is edible, from top to bottom. It provides a huge amount of nutrition. The young leaves are taken as they sprout from the plant before they fully open. Bundles of young leaf stems can be tied together and allowed to yellow. The crystals that form on the side of the plant material is rich in sugar and makes a brilliant sweetener. Note: Do not get confused with the Giant Hogweed – which is a huge plant that can cause the blistering of sensitive skin.

Steamed hogweed shoots

Collect new shoots of hogweed and remove the hairiness with a sharp knife. You can add other vegetables with this, Ransomes, chives, spring onion. Steam for ten to fifteen minutes and serve with a knob of butter.

Horseradish

This hot herb is used to make that beef accompaniment, made from the root and when strong makes you cry. The plant is completely usable. Being a radish it contains the sulphurous compounds common to these plants. The leaves and stems, which are thick and floppy, taste less hot than the root.

Scrub and peel the root and grate with the fine grater (watch your fingers!) Then you can make the sauce by adding hot milk and cornflour or simply cream for crème fraiche.

Wild Fennel

This is an escapee from gardens which crops up all over the place and is taking over many habitats. The leaves and bulb can be used, although it is most usually grown for the bulb. You will find that the wild type is disappointing when it comes to the bulb, the root takes over and it is fibrous and harsh. However it can be used to some extent in a purée mixed with mayonnaise. Please remember our rules about uprooting wild plants.

Barbecueing with Fennel

If you gather a lot of fennel leaves and place them on top of the BBQ (over the grill) you will find that the fish placed on the smouldering fennel cooks evenly and takes on an excellent smoky aniseed flavour. It is particularly good with fish, and you can finely chop a few leaves and mix with crème fraiche.

Salmon with Fennel

Ingredients
1 washed and gutted salmon
500g (1lb) fennel leaves
25g (1oz) butter
4 crushed garlic cloves of a hand full of chopped Ransoms
1 sliced lemon

You will need a fish kettle or large pan.

Finely chop the fennel leaves and incorporate with the butter and garlic.

Stuff the fish with the mixture and wrap tightly in cling film. You can sew up the fish if you wish.

Place in the kettle adding boiling water and the lemon slices and cook at the rate of 6 minutes per pound of fish. If your fish is over 8 pounds, give it an extra simmer for another 6 minutes.

Courgette

This isn't a wild plant, but does turn up now near gardens and allotments, and is a truly wonderful plant. In the wild their fruit is not so good, but the flowers are ideal for stuffing.

Stuffed turnip and cheese courgettes

Ingredients
10 courgette flowers
5 shallots
500g (1lb) turnips
250g (0.5lb) Really mature chedder cheese

Peel and chop the turnips so they are 1 cm cubes and par boil them for 3 minutes. Finely chop the shallots and grate the cheese. When the turnips are cooled incorporate all the ingredients together and bake in a hot (200°C degrees, Gas 6) oven for ten minutes.

Wild Chives

This plant is a godsend in the kitchen. You can keep going back to it, cropping every few days – just enough for your use. The flowers make an edible garnish too!

The round leaves are full of juice and flavour that just a few are needed for an excellent onion flavour.

Chives omelette

I know, making an omelette is easy – but making a good one is a special skill.

Ingredients
3 fresh free range eggs
1 handful of chopped chives
1 handful of chopped Ransoms (or 2 crushed chopped garlic cloves)
Large knob of butter

Place your pan on a high heat and add the butter.

When melted, reduce the heat by half and add half the chives, and all the garlic/ ransoms.

Beat the eggs vigourously to incorporate as much air as possible and pour into the pan.

Reduce the heat to low and leave the omelette to cook undisturbed.

Once set on the bottom, sprinkle the rest of the chives into the pan and place under the grill to finish the top so that it is as light as a souffle.

Edible weeds & flowers

Mountain Ash – Sorbus scopulina

Part used
Only the fruit and is a very old foodstuff.

Type of dish
Cooked fruit, rowan jelly, jams and preserves.

Information
Bitter seeds can contain cyanide in minute quantities.

Yellow Ashphodel – Asphodeline lutea

Part used
Roots, young shoots and flowers.

Type of dish
Roast root. Shoots boiled fairly bland. Flowers are sweet.

Information
Easy to grow plant with no health problems.

Bell flower – Campanula alliariifolia

Part used
Leaves and flowers.

Type of dish
Cooked to make a vegetable or eaten raw in salads.

Information
Slightly bitter, use sparingly.

Borage – Borago officinalis

Part used
Leaves and flowers.

Type of dish
Leaves, raw or cooked in salads.
Flowers are sweet.

Information
Used in Pimms.
Do not take if you have liver problems.

Opium poppy – Papaver somniferum

Part used
Seeds.

Type of dish
Brilliant nutty flavour, can be used instead of sesame.

Information
In the UK the hallucinogenic chemicals do not appear.

Red clover – Trifolium pratense

Part used
Leaves and flowers.

Type of dish
Leaves are used in salads and soups, flowers in teas.

Information
Do not take the seeds as they will cause tummy upset.

Creeping thistle – Cirsium arvense

Part used
Leaves, roots and stem.

Type of dish
Leaves are trimmed and boiled. Stems are peeled and steamed.

Information
Not much flavour but is nutritious. Use with other veg.

Ground elder – Aegopodium podagraria

Part used
Leaves

Type of dish
Leaves are used cooked in stews or to make a vegetable dish.

Information
Tangy flavour, not well liked by many.

Hedge garlic – Allaria petiolata

Part used
Leaves.

Type of dish
Used in salads mostly. Sometimes used to flavour stews.

Information
Not a true garlic.

Oak –
Quercus robur

Part used
Fruit.

Type of dish
Ground and soaked in water, used in bread making or coffee.

Information
Do not take raw, soak in many changes of water.

Rape –
Brassica napus napus

Part used
Leaves, stems and sprouted seeds.

Type of dish
Stems cooked like broccoli. Leaves are boiled as cabbage.

Information
Avoid raw seeds, Sprouted ones resemble mustard.

Cow Parsley –
Anthriscus sylvestris

Part used
Leaves.

Type of dish
The leaves are cooked to create a stew. Flavourless raw.

Information
Related to hemlock, which has purple blotches on the stem.

Mahonia –
Mahonia fremontii

Part used
Flowers and fruit.

Type of dish
Fruit is usually cooked and is full of seed. Flowers can be collected to make a cordial.

Information

Pleasant flavour from such a harsh looking plant.

Rosebay willowherb –
Epilobium sp.

Part used
Flowers, leaves and stems.

Type of dish
Considered an excellent asparagus type veg. Raw leaves in salads.

Information
Also used to make tea.

Also used to make tea.

Snowberry –
Gaultheria hispidula

Part used
Fruit.

Type of dish
Eaten raw or cooked. They have a pleasant flavour of witch hazel.

Information
Can make a cordial from the fruit.

Dead nettle –
Lamium album

Part used
Leaves and flowers.

Type of dish
Eaten raw in salads.

Information
They look like nettles but are not, hence the name.

Nasturtium –
Tropaelum major

Part used
Leaves, stems, flowers and fruit.

Type of dish
All the plant is used in salads.

Information
Fruits are an excellent caper substitute. Leaves are nutty and succulent.

Chickweed –
Cerastium fontanum

Part used
Leaves and young stems.

Type of dish
Raw in salads, stems cooked like spinach.

Information
Easy to grow and collect. Surprisingly pleasant.

Hawthorn –
Cretagus sp.

Part used
Fruit.

Type of dish
Succulent fruit is either cooked, dried or eaten raw.

Information
Can be added to pork pies!

Fat hen –
Cheonopodium album

Part used
Leaves, flowers and stems.

Type of dish
Raw or cooked, this plant makes an excellent green vegetable.

Information
Only take the young stems, the older ones are unpleasant.

Wild mint –
Mentha sp.

Part used
Leaves.

Type of dish
Added to salads or picked for tea or added to stews, a most useful plant.

Information
Be careful during pregnancy, some reports of induced abortion exist.

Dandelion –
Taraxacum officinalis

Part used
Leaves, (Flowers in wine).

Type of dish
Leaves, raw or cooked in salads or as a spinach like vegetable.

Information
Only use fresh leaves.

Rose –
Rosa sp

Part used
Petals, shoots and fruit.

Type of dish
Petals are eaten raw, shoots are peeled and cooked. Jam is made from the fruit.

Information
Fruit is packed with Vitamin C. Do not eat the hairs inside the fruit.

Honeysuckle –
Lonicera angustifolium

Part used
Fruit.

Type of dish
These sweet fruits are eaten raw.

Information
Don't eat too many of them in one sitting.

Shepherd's purse – Capsella bursa-pastoris

Part used
Leaves.

Type of dish
Peppery, brilliant in salads. You need a lot of them to make a good meal.

Information
The seedpods can be used as a peppery condiment.

Japanese knotweed – Polygonium japonicum lutea

Part used
Young shoots.

Type of dish
Boiled young shoots make an asparagus substitute.

Information
Do not eat in large quantities—Oxalic acid can bind essential vitamins and cause illness.

Mallow – Lavatera sp

Part used
Leaves.

Type of dish
Raw or cooked, the leaves are pleasantly flavoured.

Information
Quite tough, you will wonder why you bothered.

Elderberry

Part used
Fruit, leaves, flowers

Type of dish
Flower fritters, leaf teas, wines, cordials and fruit pies.

Information
Folklore says you should never sleep under this plant because you might be transported into the world of the fairies.

Wild chives

Part used
Leaves and flowers

Type of dish
Used as a condiment or flavouring in omelettes, salads and stews.

Informartion
The onion flavour contains many health giving sulphonamide type chemicals.

Edible plants from a watery world

By Anouchka Warren

The seashore

Although it's popularity is increasing, many people only come across seaweed at their local Chinese takeaway and this is a shame because it is very nutritious and is still very abundant.

There are also many different varieties and none is known to be poisonous, although some do taste better than others. One of the most commonly eaten in Chinese, Korean and Japanese cuisine is Nori (Porphora). It's the same to our "Laver", a traditional food in Wales and Ireland. Whatever it's called it can be found on rugged, coastlines around the UK, mainly on the western coasts and where it can attach itself to embedded rocks. It's rich in protein, iodine, and vitamins and is very low in calories.

This has made it popular as a health food but it's often presented in the shops in tablet form which seems like such a waste. The traditional Welsh recipe is to boil it for several hours until it becomes a spinachy puree which is usually then rolled in oatmeal, fried and named Laverbread. The paste can also be used like a savoury jam or a chutney-type accompaniment to meat. But why mess with it so much? Lava bread makes an excellent addition to your usual full English breakfast, simply boiled, dried, pressed together and fried with bacon and eggs.

The way to recognise Porphora is that it looks like a green-brown tissue with a rubbery consistency. It should not be collected from anywhere but the wildest, cleanest environments. Sadly, these days, almost all our supplies come from Japan.

Samphire comes in many forms on the shore, this lonely rock grown specimen will eventually grow into a large plant.

Further inland

Bilberries grow abundantly around beachy areas, mainly further north in Britain. They're small branched shrubs, with wiry angular branches, rarely over a foot high, and the black berries, which are blackcurrant-sized are covered with a grey, misty bloom when ripe. The leaves which are leathery can be used in tea. The berries are best cooked, but don't need much sugar added to make lovely jam or tart filling with a rich colour and flavour.

Sea Kale may be in decline but it is still commonly found growing at the tops of pebbled beaches

Sea Kale is unfortunately declining in Britain because of sea-defence work but can still be found. It grows in large clumps of grey-green leaves with purple stalks, and in summer with clusters of white flowers which smell sweet and attract insects. As with all plants it's best to choose young shoots and leaves, but the stems of Sea Kale in particular can become quite woody and tough as they get older. The plants can be found near the top of the beach growing on shingle or pebbles. Shoots, if young can be blanched and then either eaten raw or steamed and buttered. Thick leaves and underground stems can be boiled and eaten and taste a bit like cabbage.

Look for Wall Pepper growing on and inbetween rocks

Wall Pepper which grows on rocks and shingle tastes sharp and peppery and the leaves can be eaten raw as a salad or cooked and used to flavour soup. Summer Purslane grows in salt marshes below the high-tide mark. The leaves can be picked at any time of year and simmered in water and flavoured with lemon juice as an accompaniment to other plants and food.

Into the estuary

Elsewhere in this book you will find recipes for Samphire, that extremely popular vegetable being served in expensive restaurants around the country. But where the river meets the sea a huge amount of life exists. Zostera is a grass which is used in Chinese cooking, and is harvested in Norway in millions of tonnes each year, looks like a grass growing in the water. Its other name is Eel Grass, and is quite edible.

Further up the river, the Common Reedmace (many of you will know it as a bulrush) has been eaten for centuries. The whole fruit was eaten, though the reed itself was dried out and soaked in animal fat to make a special candle called a reed light. These were much preferred to candles for many because they were cheaper and gave out a better light.

Summer

Gooseberries

Jams and jellies

Elderflowers

Crayfish

Watercress

Rose petals

Wild strawberries

Country wines

Fresh water fish

12th August

Blackberries

Cobnuts

Wild fruit yoghurt

Elderberries

Gooseberries galore

Vanessa Kendell greets the gorgeous gooseberry

Gooseberries mark the start of the British berry season. They have that delightful mixture of tartness and juiciness making them a wonderfully versatile ingredient in the kitchen. Some are better disposed towards a gentle stewing; other varieties (and there are countless) are sweet and can be eaten raw. They thrive in our climate and are relatively easy to grow, and often found growing wild.

One reason the gooseberry is often neglected is its lack of spontaneity. Unlike other berries, the gooseberry demands to be cooked and sweetened before announcing itself palatable. But there is very little to do once you pluck them from their punnets: simply throw the lime-veined little orbs into a pan with a splash of water and a generous amount of brown sugar to balance the sharpness. Once lightly stewed in this way, the flavour turns from one of unpleasant astringency to a lush mellowness. The softened berries can be folded into whipped double cream, spread over warm scones, sandwiched in a Victoria sponge or piled into baked buttery pastry. The high pectin content will reward you with excellent jam and jelly, plus they freeze particularly well.

And its talents don't stop there. It is said the gooseberry gets its name from the fact that its acidic flesh makes a superb sauce to serve alongside goose, not to mention that, traditionally, the first appearance of goose at dinner tables was at Whitsuntide, coinciding with the start of the gooseberry season. Its fresh, tangy notes are perfect for cutting through rich and fatty meat. Furthermore, its French name, groseille à maquereau, implies that mackerel would be lost without it.

Wait a few weeks, though, and the mature yellow and red varieties have an obvious sweetness which makes them superb eaten straight off the bush. What other berry can claim to have this much going for it?

●

Baked mackerel with pilaf stuffing and gooseberry sauce

This makes a rather impressive main course served with a simple tomato salad. You may well have more pilaf than the mackerel can take, in which case just serve it in a bowl on the table for those who want extra.

Serves 6

6 medium mackerel, backbones removed
Butter, for greasing

For the gooseberry sauce:
250g (9oz) gooseberries, topped and tailed
Zest and juice of 1 lemon
1 tbsp caster sugar
5 tbsp water
Salt and freshly ground black pepper

For the pilaf:
500g (1lb) basmati rice
30g (1oz) unsalted butter
3 shallots, chopped
6 cardamom pods, crushed
½ tsp ground cinnamon
Pinch of ground cloves
About 650ml (just over 1 pint) hot vegetable stock
1 tsp salt
Freshly ground black pepper
75g (2-3oz) pine nuts, toasted in a dry pan

METHOD
Start by making the pilaf. Rinse the rice under cold water until the water runs clear, then leave to soak for 30 minutes or an hour if you have the time.

Melt the butter in a large pan and fry the shallots until browned and caramelised. Add all the spices to the pan and fry gently for a minute or so. Stir the drained rice into the spices and fry for a few minutes to coat the grains in the spiced onions. Pour in the hot stock, season with salt and pepper and bring to the boil. Turn the heat down, then simmer over a low heat for

15-20 minutes or until the liquid is absorbed.

Meanwhile, put the gooseberries in a saucepan with the lemon zest and juice, sugar and water. Bring to the boil, then simmer very gently for 10-15 minutes until completely soft. Push the pulp through a sieve, so you end up with a purée. Taste and season with salt and pepper. Leave to cool slightly. Preheat the oven

to 190° (375°F, gas 5).

Turn the cooked rice out into a bowl and pick out the cardamom pods. Fork through the toasted pine nuts. Stuff the mackerel with the pilaf and place in a greased baking dish. Cover with foil and bake in the oven for 20-25 minutes. Serve the mackerel drizzled with the gooseberry sauce.

Gooseberry yoghurt sorbet

A yoghurt sorbet is one of the easiest things to make, plus it's divinely creamy without the heaviness a custard-based ice cream can have. Folding in a mass of cooked gooseberries is really no extra effort – provided you can get someone else to top and tail them, of course.

Serves 4-6

300g (11oz) gooseberries, topped and tailed
3 tbsp water
2 tbsp caster sugar
Squeeze of lemon juice
500g Greek yoghurt (large tub)
3-4 tbsp unrefined golden icing sugar

METHOD
Tumble the gooseberries into a large pan and add the water and caster sugar. Cover and simmer very gently for 10-15 minutes until the gooseberries are completely soft. Add a squeeze of lemon juice, then push the pulp through a sieve, so you end up with a purée. Leave to cool slightly.

Mix the yoghurt and gooseberry purée together in a bowl and beat in three tablespoons of icing sugar. Taste and add more if necessary. All that remains is to churn the mixture in an ice-cream machine. Simple.

If you don't have an ice-cream machine, pour the mixture into a freezer-proof container and freeze for four hours. Take it out and beat it. Return to freezer and repeat after another three hours.

Gooseberry and sultana chutney

A good chutney to serve with cheese, cold meats and crumbly pork pies.

Makes about 1kg

500g (1lb) gooseberries, topped and tailed
200g (7oz) sultanas
2 large onions, sliced
450ml (¾ pint) white wine vinegar
250g (9oz) light muscovado sugar
1 tsp mustard seeds
1 tsp ground ginger
1 tsp ground allspice
1 tsp salt

METHOD
Put all the ingredients into a preserving pan or large, heavy-based pan and bring slowly to the boil, stirring occasionally to dissolve the sugar. Simmer for 45 minutes to an hour until the mixture has reduced and thickened. Stir now and again to prevent sticking.

Pour the hot chutney into warm, sterilised jars and seal with plastic-coated lids. Leave to mature for several weeks before eating.

Gooseberry crème brûlée

This might seem an excessive amount of demerara sugar on top of what is already in the custard and gooseberries, but you do need a lovely thick crust of blistered sugar to give that satisfying crack.

Serves 6

Knob of butter
300g (11oz) gooseberries, topped and tailed
3 tbsp water
6 tbsp caster sugar
8 egg yolks
1 vanilla pod
600ml (1 pint) double cream
6 tbsp demerara sugar

METHOD
Melt the butter in a large pan and add the gooseberries. Cover and cook gently for a few minutes, then add the water and half the caster sugar. Simmer over a very low heat for 10-15 minutes until the gooseberries are soft. Divide between six ramekins, then chill.

Beat the egg yolks and remaining caster sugar in a bowl until pale. Split the vanilla pod down the middle and scrape the seeds into a saucepan. Add the vanilla pod and cream and heat until just on the verge of coming up to the boil, then pour the warmed cream over the egg yolks, whisking as you do so. Return the mixture to the saucepan and cook over a low heat for 15-20 minutes, stirring, until the custard is very thick.

Pour the custard into the chilled ramekins, leave to cool, then refrigerate for a good few hours or overnight. Sprinkle with demerara sugar and caramelise using a blowtorch or under a hot grill.

Spiced gooseberry sauce

An excellent accompaniment for goose, this spiced gooseberry sauce will also sit nicely with roast pork, especially old-fashioned pork which comes with layers of glorious fat.

Serves 4

250g (9oz) gooseberries, topped and tailed
Zest and juice of 1 lemon
1 tbsp light muscovado sugar
5 tbsp water
Pinch of ground cinnamon
Grated nutmeg
Salt and freshly ground black pepper

METHOD
Put the gooseberries in a saucepan with the lemon zest and juice, sugar, water, cinnamon and a generous grating of nutmeg. Bring to the boil, then simmer very gently for 10-15 minutes until softened.

The sauce is not intended to be too sweet, but if the tartness proves too much, add a little more sugar. Season with salt and pepper and serve.

Jams and jellies – the basics

Equipment and materials needed for preserving with sugar to make jams, conserves and bottled fruit

Picture Chris Graham

One of the easiest ways to preserve your wild fruit harvest is by turning it into jams and jellies. If you have never done this before, don't be put off by the talk of preserving pans and jelly-bag stands, pectin levels and setting temperatures – it isn't as complicated as it sounds! The basic idea is that fruit is simmered to extract the pectin and then sugar is added. This combination is then boiled for a while to reduce the water content and left to set in sterile jars. That doesn't sound too difficult does it?

The difference between jam and jelly is that jams contain flesh from the fruit but jellies are made from the strained, cooked juice and so are clear and smooth in texture. Some fruit, like crab-apples, are more suited to jelly-making than others as they set better. What determines how well jams set, are the acid and pectin contents of the fruit, and the proportion of sugar used.

Acidity can be increased by the addition of lemon juice, acid juice from other fruit, like gooseberries or redcurrants, which have naturally high levels, or citric acid dissolved in water. As a rough guide, the acidity in the fruit you use, wants to roughly equal the acidity tasted when one tablespoonful of freshly squeezed lemon juice is added to half a cup of water.

Pectin is a gelling-agent, which occurs naturally in plants, and it's this which is extracted by the cooking process and thickens the jam. To test the pectin level, after simmering the fruit take a spoonful of the juice out of the pan and drop it into a cold glass. Add three teaspoonfuls of methylated spirit and shake. A firmish, gluey blob will form if the level is good and high. A few smaller, less well-formed lumps means the level is only just alright, and lots of little wobbly ones means there is not enough. This is easy to rectify.

Preserving sugar can be bought in most supermarkets and this already contains pectin, or you can buy it in liquid form in bottles. Alternatively, you can make your own by simmering pectin-rich fruit such as green apples, redcurrants or gooseberries to extract theirs, and then adding as much juice as you need to your jam to achieve a good set. Lemon juice and pith also work well for this, added at a rate of the juice of four lemons to every 1.8kg of fruit, before cooking starts. The pith should be put into a muslin bag (a scalded cotton handkerchief tied with string is a good substitute) and cooked with everything else, then removed before potting. The easiest way to make sure you have enough pectin though, is to add fruit which have high levels to your main flavour. This is how some classic combinations have arisen – ripe apples are naturally low in pectin, blackberries naturally high, hence blackberry and apple jam, the same for pear and gooseberry, strawberry and redcurrant and so on. ●

What do you need?

Pans

Preserving pans are just large, heavy-based pans usually with a lip for pouring, which will allow the fruit and sugar to heat to the right temperature without 'catching' (sticking to the bottom of the pan and burning). If you are planning on making a lot of jam, then it is probably worth investing in one. If it's only the occasional pot, just use the heaviest pan you have.

Jelly-bags

These are simply very fine-meshed bags used to drain the juice out of the cooked pulp, if you want to make jelly instead of jam. You can buy them complete with a stand, or you can make your own and use a scalded glass-cloth or muslin, hung up with string to the handle of one of your top kitchen cupboards, so the juice drips into a bowl on the worktop. The only rule with either of these is… whatever you do, don't try to hurry the process and squeeze the juice out, or it'll go cloudy. Be patient and let it drip overnight.

Jars and lids

Old jam jars can be kept, thoroughly washed and re-used. If this doesn't appeal to you, new jars may be bought, either individually or in packs. Replacement lids are available too and are probably a good idea, just in case your second-hand ones have been dented or distorted. The last thing you want is for air to get in and ruin your hard work!

Thermometer

Whatever you do, don't use a normal medical thermometer! Jam thermometers are undoubtedly useful and can be used for other things too, like yoghurt or, even better, fudge and toffee. It is possible to make jam without one and involves fairly constant checking of the consistency towards the end, by putting a teaspoonful onto a cold plate, leaving it to set and seeing how it is by pushing it with your fingertip. When ready, the skin will wrinkle as you move it. Far easier to have a thermometer!

Equipment available from:
www.lakelandlimited.com
www.ascott.biz

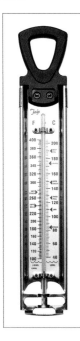

Pictures courtesy Lakeland Limited

Jam funnel

When pouring hot jam into jars, it is both easier and safer, to use a wide-necked jam funnel. These are cheap and, while not essential, I would recommend you use one. Jam is ready at 104-105°C and its sugar content makes sure it sticks to you if it spills. Better safe than sorry I think.

Sugar

For most jams and jellies, plain white granulated sugar is fine. At the peak of the season, supermarkets even bring in the big 5kg bags to cater for jam-makers which certainly is handy. Preserving sugar, as mentioned above, has added pectin, so if you are using fruit you know to be low in pectin this is probably the best option. Other sugars can be used, but will lend their own flavour to the jam. This could be used to an advantage, imagine fig jam with a hint of treacly dark Muscovado…

Fruit

The fruit you choose should be firm and only just ripe. Any over-ripeness will reduce the setting quality. Large fruit should be wiped clean, berries and smaller fruit can be rinsed under a tap in a colander and left to drain. If wet fruit is used, the additional water can mess up the calculations. Don't use any fruit, which are mouldy, diseased or over-ripe. Skins, stalks and leaves need to be removed for jam, but can be left on if you are making jelly, as the straining process will remove any solids.

Basic jam recipe

Every 1.8kg of fruit will make about 10 pots of jam. Wash your jars and lids before you start, make sure they are dry and put them onto a baking tray and into a warm oven to heat up.

1.8kg (4lb) blackberries
1.8kg (4lb) sugar
150ml (0.25 pint) water
4 tablespoons lemon juice, pith in a bag

Simmer the berries and lemon juice and pith for 8-10 minutes. Add the sugar and boil hard til either the mixture comes up to temperature on a sugar thermometer or until a teaspoonful sets on a plate. Remove from the heat and leave to cool for 7-8 minutes, then carefully pour into the warm jars and do the lids up. Leave to cool then label. Store in a cool dark place.

Basic jelly

1.8kg (4lb) washed blackberries
450ml (0.75 pint) water
4 tablespoons (20 fl oz) lemon juice
450g (1lb) sugar to each 600ml of juice

Simmer the fruit in the water for ¾-1 hour to cook the fruit and extract all the juice. Mash the fruit as it cooks to help release juice. Test for pectin and if necessary, add lemon juice. Strain overnight through a scalded jelly bag. Measure the volume of juice extracted, return to pan and add 450g of sugar for every 600ml of juice. Boil rapidly – it will come to setting point faster than jam. You will see some scum on the surface, don't worry about this, just clear it away with a large spoon. Pot as for jam, but make sure you are quick, or the jelly will start to set in the pan.

The magic of the Elder
(Sambucus nigra)

Without question, the elder is the most useful of all wild plants. It is an all year around source of a key ingredient to a wide variety of recipes, as **Peter Litfoot** explains

While not a particularly large tree, the elder is a very fast growing tree. Most of the time it's not a particularly attractive tree and it doesn't smell too good if you brush past one either. It has the habit of losing some branches to the extent that you may think the tree has in fact died. But in most cases, come the spring the tree bursts back into life shooting up new branches producing a profusion of flowers in May or June followed by berries later from late July to October.

Elders are found in hedgerows, in woodlands, in ditches beside streams and in open spaces in and around farm land. At home we have many of them growing through cracks in the concrete around disused buildings and even have one growing out of the side of our house. The flower buds, flowers and the berries are commonly collected for consumption, as are the fungi that often grow on the decaying branches. However, do not think of eating the leaves or the wood, they are poisonous.

Away with the fairies?

This is a tree that has been valuable to man for thousands of years. There are many myths about it, cutting one down was thought to be unlucky. Sitting under the tree on midsummers night was said to summon the appearance of fairies – not sure how long it took for people to work out they were on a hiding to nothing here! But at least the plant also helps drive away witches and protect you from whatever nasty disease happens to be doing the rounds. And forget about all those expensive facial creams, all you need to do is douse yourself in distilled elderflower water!

We should perhaps dismiss all the myths, the plant is clearly credited for many herbal qualities. The flowers are thought to have many medicinal uses when made into a herbal tea. These include treatment of colds and flues, urinary infections, rheumatism and headaches. The berries are rich in vitamin C and other vitamins that are well known to be good for boosting the immune system. Anti oxidants, which are present in some quantities, are widely recommended to slow down the aging process. They are also reported to be good for sore throats, catarrh, coughs, colds, bronchitis and asthma.

Flowers

The flowers can be made into a very simple

"...widely recommended to slow down the aging process"

and tasty cordial and also into wine, champagne and vinegar. They go well stewed with gooseberries or rhubarb. They are sometimes used to flavour jams and jellies, and eaten on there own fried in batter, elderflower fritters are very popular. While generally a wild plant, the flowers are collected commercially in some areas, you can purchase elderflower cordial in most supermarkets.

Berries

Elder berries can be added to any other fruit to make puddings, jams or soft drinks and smoothies. Elderberry wine is probably the most popular home made country wine, and rightly so. The berries act as a laxative and a diuretic and eating them raw in large quantities can bring on nausea, so don't eat too many all at once!

Fungi

The Jew's Ear Fungus which commonly grows on the decaying branches of the elder is one of the very few frost tolerant species of edible fungus helping to make it available all year around, although in very dry spells it may be harder to find. It's easy to identify and good to eat. It can easily be dried and stored and can also be purchased from many health food shops. We will look at this fungus in more detail later.

Growing

It may or may not be unlucky to cut down an Elder tree, but if you do cut it down, unless you remove the roots, it's most likely to grow back again. You've probably come to the conclusion that it's certainly lucky if you do have them close at hand. However, even if you do not, they are certainly very easy to grow.

I once chopped down a whole load of elder trees, trying to clear an entrance to an old building. The branches were left discarded on the ground for a couple of weeks before I decided they would make the perfect supports for my young pea plants. By the time all the peas were harvested, and the pea plants thrown into the compost heap, roughly half of the elder branches had grown roots and were sprouting a healthy fresh growth of leaves.

So, if you want to add this plant into your garden, or you want to simply grow more of them, collect up some branches, pull off all of the side shoots and use them, instead of bamboo, for supporting the growth of your tomatoes, beans or peas! •

Elder buds, available from April to May can be eaten raw or fried in batter

The flowers grow in profusion, pick as many as you need, you should still be blessed with enough berries later in the year

The small berries should be picked when fully ripe. They can be frozen for future use if you have a surplus

The little flowers are delicate and to keep the flavour they should not be washed. Do not pick them if they look damaged or discoloured

Use elder branches instead of bamboo when growing your vegetables. They're perfectly up for the job and you should end up with new elder trees

It may look all ear like and feel all rubbery, but this fungi is well worth harvesting

Elderflowers

Lucy Young, author of *Secrets from a Country Kitchen* (Ebury Press) and *Aga Easy* (Absolute Press) makes the most of this seasonal treat

This is such a perfect time of year for collecting elderflowers. They are growing in abundance in the hedgerows in early June, fantastic tiny, cream-coloured flowers speckling the large flat heads. The smell is just wonderful, lovely fresh and lemony.

Elderflowers are often used as a herbal remedy, to fight against colds and summer 'flu and as an anti-catarrhal remedy and for hayfever sufferers. Use the heads to make a refreshing tea, mixed with lemon balm, lemon zest or with peppermint leaves. Simply pop them into a teapot (loose) and pour over boiling water, leave for a minute or two and strain to serve hot or cold. Alternatively, elderflower cordial is the best way to preserve this taste of summer, and is surprisingly easy to make.

Preparation

Pick from the hedgerows and shake well to remove any flies. Carefully wash in water (do not saturate) and dry gently in a salad spinner or tea towel. Keep in poly-bag in the fridge for up to a week. If you have picked too many to make the cordial all at once, the heads can be frozen.

The most successful way to use the heads is to make the cordial and then use as a refreshing drink with fizzy water or mixed with apple juice and fizzy water. The cordial can then be used as an ingredient in recipes. Elderflowers are a natural partner to gooseberries too and really enhance their flavour.

•

Elderflower glazed pineapple with rum and ginger

This lovely recipe is low in fat – but only if you follow my suggestion of serving it with crème fraîche! You can use Malibu or brandy if you prefer them to rum.

Serves 4
Preparation time 10 minutes
Cooking time 15 minutes
Not suitable for freezing

1 medium just ripe fresh pineapple
3 tbsp dark rum
6 tbsp elderflower cordial
4 tbsp water
3 bulbs stem ginger from a jar, finely chopped

METHOD
Remove the top from the pineapple. Peel and cut in four lengthways. Remove the core and cut each quarter lengthways into four long wedges (giving you 16 strips).

Place the pineapple wedges into a wide-based saucepan (so they are in a single layer). Pour over the other ingredients, except the chopped stem ginger, cover, and bring to the boil. Lower the heat and simmer (do not allow to boil) for about 15 minutes until just tender – the pineapple still wants to hold its shape and be just tender to eat.

Transfer the pineapple to a serving dish, and sprinkle over the stem ginger. Reduce the sauce a little, to a thin coating consistency, and pour over the pineapple.

Serve four wedges per person (making sure every plate has stem ginger too). Pour a little sauce over the top, and add a dollop of crème fraîche if you like.

To cook in the Aga
Bring the pan to simmering point on the simmering plate, cover and transfer to the simmering oven for about 15 minutes until just tender.

Lucy's Tip
If a pineapple is ripe, it will smell sweet. If you can pull a leaf out easily from the top, this is a sign of ripeness too. I have served these warm or cold, and both are equally as delicious. If serving cold, they can be made up to 24 hours ahead. Stem ginger is bought in a jar in syrup, be sure not to confuse it with fresh or crystallised ginger.

Elderflower cordial

Store as a cordial in the refrigerator for up to three months. Or freeze the cordial and defrost to use.

1.7kg (3½lb) granulated sugar
1.5 litres (2½ pints) water
3 lemons
About 25 elderflower heads
50g (2oz) citric acid (sold in pharmacies or suppliers of home-brewing equipment)

METHOD
Measure the sugar and water into a large pan, bring to the boil stirring until the sugar has dissolved. Remove from the heat and cool. Slice the lemons thinly by hand or in the processor, and put into a large polythene box or bowl. Add the elderflower heads and citric acid to the lemons and pour over the cool syrup. Cover and leave overnight.

Strain through a sieve into a jug. Strain again through muslin into bottles and store the cordial in the fridge.

To serve as Elderflower Champagne (non alcoholic) – dilute to taste with chilled fizzy water and ice.

Makes about 2½ – 3 pints

Lucy's Tip

The elderflower heads can be frozen once picked. Freeze in poly-bags in 25-head quantities and plunge into sugar syrup straight from the freezer – do not defrost first otherwise the syrup will go slimy.

Elderflower and gooseberry fool

This is a fool made in the classical way, but one that is lighter in fat because I have used a proportion of low-fat crème fraîche. It can also be made with other fruits when in season. I think it looks best served in cocktail or wine glasses.

Serves 4
Preparation time 10 minutes
Cooking time 10 minutes
Not suitable for freezing

900g (2lb) fresh gooseberries, topped and tailed
2 tablespoons elderflower cordial
100g (4oz) caster sugar
1 x 200 ml (7floz) carton half-fat crème fraîche
300ml (10floz) double cream, lightly whipped
Fresh elderflower petals or mint leaves, to garnish

METHOD
Measure the prepared fruit into a large saucepan with the elderflower cordial and sugar, and cover with a lid. Simmer over a low heat for about 10 minutes, or until the gooseberries are soft, stirring occasionally.

Sieve the gooseberries over a large bowl so only the skin and seeds remain in the sieve (discard these). Carefully stir the crème fraîche into the gooseberry pulp, then fold in the whipped cream.

Spoon into four large wine glasses and chill (it will not set firm, but it will thicken up a little). Decorate with elderflower petals or fresh mint leaves, and serve chilled.

To cook in the Aga
Cook the gooseberries, elderflower cordial and sugar, covered, in the simmering oven for about 10 minutes until soft.

Lucy's Tip
If you like texture, you do not need to sieve the gooseberries. I'm not keen on pips or skin, which is why I sieve them. If you haven't made your elderflower cordial yet, use apple juice or water instead.

Floating garden punch

This is perfect for those lazy summer evenings. Quick to make and so refreshing too, the cucumber and elderflower looks stunning floating in a large glass jug.

Serves 4-6
Preparation time 5 mins

8 tablespoons vodka
8 tablespoons elderflower cordial
600 ml (1 pint) soda water
½ cucumber, skin on
Fresh elderflower sprigs

METHOD
To make, measure equal quantities of vodka and elderflower cordial into a jug and add soda water to taste.

Cut thin slices of cucumber and cut again into quarters and drop into punch with a few elderflower sprigs.

Add ice and serve immediately.

Crayfish

Deep within the rivers of the UK a strange form of biological warfare has been taking place, and we have not been doing too well. The native freshwater crayfish, the white clawed crayfish, has plummeted in numbers whereas the American usurper has been busy taking its place in our rivers.

The major problem is crayfish plague, which is a disease caused by a fungus carried by the American species. It does not affect them at all, but decimates the native crayfish.

Many rivers and canals have a real crayfish problem, and it is illegal to put the American ones back once caught. They are easy to catch with a fishing line with some bacon on the hook; just like crabbing. In a river where there are a lot of crayfish you will catch half a dozen really quickly. You need at least this many. You can also buy a crayfish trap in which you will collect a dozen or more overnight.

Once caught, keep them in fresh water for at least a day to flush out their system and then put them into the fridge on ice to bring them into a state of torpor. This is the most humane way of killing them and is recommended by the RSPCA. Once they no longer respond to stimuli, drop them quickly into boiling water, when they will die straight away.

There is only two possible sources of meat on crayfish. Remove the tails and flick out the meat it contains. You might wish to remove the dark line which is the gut. Also, break open the claws. You can use this meat as you require.

Creamy crayfish

Ingredients

500g (1lb) crayfish meat
1 large onion
2 garlic cloves crushed and shredded
25g (1oz) grated ginger
150ml (¼pint) double cream
100g (¼lb) chopped almonds
100ml (4fl oz) stock (probably best from the broth in which you cooked the crayfish)

This is good cooked in a wok.

METHOD
In a little oil, fry the onion, garlic and ginger for a couple of minutes.
Add the almonds and the stock and bring to the boil. Cook for 5 minutes. Add the crayfish meat and incorporate for another couple of minutes. Gently add the cream and mix together. Season to taste.

Watercress

Paul Peacock provides a couple of ideas for cooking watercress which, due to parasite risks, is essential if it is collected from an area where grazing animals maybe present upstream

Fast flowing beds, fed by chalk rich streams in Southern England are one of the best places to find wild watercress. So much so that the commercial producers of this wonderful vegetable have taken over huge acres of this freshwater habitat.

This plant is very commonly found in salad mixes, but is wonderful in soups and is almost impossible to better cooked with fish.

Collecting can be difficult if there are large numbers of sheep upstream, whence you would have to cook it to kill any parasites. You can, however, grow your own. It does not need running water, just damp compost in a polythene lined tray about the size of a palette. Broadcast your seed on it and leave outside. Your cress can now be eaten raw without any worry.

You can stir-fry watercress. It combines well with ginger, bean sprouts, lemon grass and pak choi. It also makes a wonderful savoury garnish.

Watercress soup

Ingredients

1 large potato
250g (½lb) watercress (large stalks removed)
1 large onion
1 carrot (Or any other root vegetable)
1 Litre (1¾pints) vegetable stock
50ml (2fl oz) cream

METHOD

Peel the vegetables and dice into small cubes. Remove the largest stalks from the watercress.

Sweat the chopped onion in a little oil and add the vegetables (not the cress)

Cook for 5 minutes.

Add the Stock and cook until the vegetables are tender. Add the cress and cook for a further 5 minutes. Blend with a hand blender and stir in the cream. Season to taste.

Peppered watercress garnish for steak

Ingredients

3 shallots
2 handfulls of fresh watercress
200ml (7fl oz) cream
Plenty of black pepper

This should be cooked in the pan in which your steak has been cooked, unwashed.

METHOD

Chop your shallots finely and fry in a little oil, mixing the juices from the steak.

Once the shallots are just beginning to caramelise, add your cress and allow to wilt. Finally add your cream and stir in continually until hot. (You might not need all the cream). Serve with a good sprinkling of freshly milled fresh black pepper.

The Queen of flowers

Not just beautiful but tasty too; as **Heather Archer** discovers, roses are just as at home in the kitchen as in the garden

The Rose is the most beautiful of all garden flowers and still by far the most popular plant in our gardens. Its history reaches back to over 300 years before the birth of Christ.

Theophrastus (c.370-286BC) wrote, in his *Enquiry into Plants*, of roses having anything from five to one hundred petals and at about the same time coins on the island of Rhodes depicted the flowers of a rose.

Preserved in monasteries in the Middle Ages for its medicinal qualities the rose began to play a prominent part in the symbolism of the church, and Edward I of England took the rose as his emblem. Remember the War of the Roses? The House of York took the white rose and the House of Lancaster the red rose as their emblems.

Medieval cooks used the highly scented damask rose petals to flavour sauces and fruit pies and for many years the rose remained an important culinary ingredient of savoury and sweet dishes, drinks and medicinal syrups.

Every part of the plant can be used, the buds, hips, leaves, bark and petals.

The beauty of the rose garden is undeniable; it lifts the spirits to walk through highly scented borders filled with wonderful specimens, little wonder that it has been proclaimed the Queen of The Flowers!

Did you know?

● During the 19th century it was proven that roses contained essential oils. Rose oil is distilled from the petals and used in aromatherapy.
● Rose hips contain high doses of vitamin C and can therefore help to ward off the common cold.
● In the 1st century Pliny the Elder recorded thirty-two different medicinal uses of the rose.
● Tincture of the Apothecary's Rose was prescribed for sore throats in 1930.
● The Native Americans used rose petals, hips and roots to treat a variety of conditions, including colds, fevers, diarrhoea, influenza and stomach troubles.
● The Flathead and Cheyenne tribes treat snow blindness with an eyewash made by boiling the petals, stem bark or root bark. The Cheyenne also boiled the inner bark to make a tea valued for treating diarrhoea and stomach trouble.

Tips:

● When using roses in the kitchen make sure that they have not been sprayed with chemicals or pesticides. Wash before use.
● Rose hips are best picked after the first frosts of winter, this makes them less bitter.
● Never eat rose hip seeds as they can irritate the digestive system.
● When making a cherry pie, sprinkle the

cherries with heavily scented rose petals before covering with pastry and baking.

● Place a handful of finely chopped heavily scented red rose petals into a jar with white sugar, seal and leave for a couple of weeks, stirring every day. The sugar will take on a pink colour and have a beautiful subtle flavour of roses. Sprinkle over scones or as the topping of a crème brulee.

● Michael Marriott, rose expert from David Austin Roses suggests using the following in your own rose 'kitchen' garden: Old roses Officinalis and Queen of Denmark and two David Austin English Roses, Gertrude Jekyll and Jude the Obscure – that's great news for me since I've just planted a Gertrude Jekyll hedge!

(Send for the lovely catalogue from David Austin Roses Limited, Bowling Green Lane, Albrighton, Wolverhampton, WV7 3HB or visit their web site www.davidaustinroses.com The new book titled The English Rose by David Austin is a great reference tool and makes a lovely gift.)

ROSE HIPS make excellent syrup and it's not a new invention either; hips were preserved in the early 18th century, as this ancient recipe shows:

Gather the hips before they grow soft. Slit in halves and take out all the seed and white that is in them; then put into an earthen pan and stir them every day… till they are soft enough to rub through a coarse hair sieve. As the pulp comes, take it off the sieve.

They are a dry berry, and will require pains to rub it through, then add its weight in sugar and mix well together without boiling, keeping it in deep gallipots for use.

ROSE WATER, distilled from damask rose petals is used to flavour sweetmeats, desserts and puddings and mixed with sugar to make an icing for sweet pies.

To **CRYSTALLISE ROSE PETALS:** Boil petals in a sugar and water syrup and set to dry individually. Decorate creamy desserts and fruit tarts, trifles and syllabubs.

"...highly scented damask rose petals..."

Rose petal sandwiches

You could cut the bread into heart shapes using a cutter and arrange on a platter dusted lightly with caster sugar and sprinkled with rose petals.

100g (4oz) butter
Handful of red or pink rose petals
8 thin slices fresh wholemeal bread

METHOD
Place the butter on a square of tin foil and completely cover with rose petals. Wrap up well to ensure the parcel is airtight and place in refrigerator overnight. Cut the crusts off the bread, spread with the fragrant butter and cover with a few fresh rose petals, cut into triangles and serve.

Rose petal and apple jelly

Delicious spread on freshly baked scones!

1kg (2.2lb) cooking apples
600ml (1 pint) water
Thinly pared rind and juice of ½ an unwaxed lemon
Granulated sugar
25-50g (1-2oz) fresh rose petals

METHOD

Peel, core and slice the apples and place in a saucepan with the water and lemon rind. Bring to the boil and simmer for about 1hr 30mins.

Strain the contents through a jelly bag and leave hanging overnight. Measure the liquid and add 225g (½lb) sugar for every ½ pint (280ml) of juice.

Put into a clean pan and add the rose petals and lemon juice. Stir over a gentle heat until the sugar has dissolved. Bring to the boil and boil rapidly for about 10 minutes. Test for setting and strain into small, warmed jars. Seal and label.

Rose petal ice cream

Delicious served with fresh strawberries or raspberries or as an accompaniment to Summer Pudding. Or simply on its own with a drizzle of Rose Hip Syrup.

500ml (¾ pint) whipped cream
4 scented deep crimson rose heads
2 large free-range eggs
200g (7oz) sugar
2 tsp honey
Pinch of ground cardamom
250ml (9fl oz) full fat milk

METHOD

Place the cream, milk, cardamom and rose petals into a saucepan and bring to just below the boil. Remove from the heat, cover and leave to infuse until cool. Whisk the egg yolks in a mixing bowl until light and fluffy. Whisk the sugar and honey, a little at a time, and then continue whisking until blended.

Strain the rose-infused milk into the egg mixture and return to the pan or double boiler. Cook very gently until slightly thickened, do not let it boil.

Chill this mixture (looks like custard now) and freeze or process in an ice cream maker. (If using an ice cream maker you could add a little rose water and fresh rose petals finely chopped). Store in the freezer.

Rose petal cordial

This is the time of year when the wild dog roses start to bloom, and the hedgerows are filled with beautiful pink flowers, the scent of which always seems much stronger than the garden variety. Pick the rose flowers when they are in full bloom and, when ready to use, pick off the petals discarding any stalks, leaves and woody bits.

METHOD

Half fill a pan with rose petals, press them down and just cover with water. Heat the water without boiling, and simmer very gently. After 30 minutes, the petals will have reduced, remove them with a sieved spoon, squeezing out any liquid. Add more petals, leaving the liquid simmering. After three or four cycles the liquid will have taken on a rich colour and scent. Pour the liquid through a fine sieve into a measuring jug and for each 100ml (3½fl oz) of warm rose water, dissolve 50g (2oz) of sugar. Bottle and keep in refrigerator.

Try making home-made ice lollies with the diluted syrup, or drizzle over ice cream.

Note: do not use shop bought or insecticide sprayed garden roses as the toxic substances cannot be removed. Choose instead wild hedgerow blooms, which have the added advantage of being readily available at no cost!

Wild Strawberries

The scientific name for the wild strawberry sounds best rolled off the tongue in an Italian accent. Fragaria sounds as though it should have come from that high alpine dolce vita world of fantastic desserts, pasta and Barolo. And so it does, but it also grows in many a British glen, and when you find them, make a meal of them as soon as you can.

Smaller, much sweeter and amazingly juicier than the cultivated strawberry, the fruits should be used in cakes and gateaux, tarts and cordials. However, there is one major problem with collecting wild strawberry fruits: it takes a willpower that, I must confess, is too much for me. I simply cannot avoid eating them straight away, within seconds of them being pulled from the plant. I start out with good intentions of personal self control but the goal of returning home with a punnet of wild strawberries eludes me. The small fruit are full of iron and potassium, and make an excellent food for people suffering from anaemia.

Thankfully there is more to this plant than its fruit. The leaves can be used in a salad, or better still, taken to make an excellent tea which has soothing antiseptic properties. It was used in Medieval times as a way of dealing with various gum diseases and was a favourite for fixing loose teeth! The roots can be used as a coffee substitute, but please do not dig them up, the return is hardly worth destroying the plant and breaking the law.

The wild strawberry tends to grow best on chalk soils, particularly in woodland, but has also been found growing quite happily on hillsides and river valleys. It can become very common in some woodland, where it spreads around the undergrowth by means of runners, throwing out new plants all over the place.

Wild strawberry butter

In Edwardian times, picnics were nothing at all without a fruit cheese or a fruit butter.

Ingredients
1kg (2¼lbs) wild strawberries
White sugar

METHOD
Wash and trim your strawberries and place them into a good heavy pan and cover with the same amount of water.

Bring to the boil and simmer until the fruit is mushy. Force the pulp through a fine sieve and weigh the amount of pulp you have.

For every 500g (1lb) pulp, you will need 250g (½lb) sugar.

Return to a pan and bring to a simmer. After around 10 minutes, stir in the appropriate amount of sugar, stirring all the time until melted. Continue to cook for another 30 minutes, at the simmer. Sterilise a sealable jar and pour the mixture and seal immediately. Allow to cool.

Wild beer and wine

It's not cooking, it's magic. Take some sugar and water and allow a micro organism, yeast, to live in it until it dies in its own excreted fluids, and when all the dead cells have fallen, drain off the clear liquid and drink it

Making country wines is the most fascinating process in the world, and one which has served mankind for thousands of generations, providing for him water in a safe form, free from diseases and other nasties. Country wines are a celebration of the fruits and plants that created them.

Country wines are nutritious. When the great temperance movements started in the Victorian Era a large number of people became malnourished because their diet, without the minerals and vitamins provided by beer and wine, was not good enough to compensate for being "tea total".

Equipment and basics

A lot of nonsense is written about the art of wine making, especially these days when so few people do it compared to yesteryear. The truth is that yeast will convert dissolved sugar into alcohol, water and carbon dioxide until such a time that the alcohol poisons the yeast or the sugar runs out, and so long as you keep everything sterile and airtight, you will not have any disappointments. The art is keeping everything simple.

To ferment wine you need two jars, each about a gallon in size and a rubber bung with an airlock in place to let the gas escape while keeping oxygen from the air out. Some flavouring; fruit juice, half a bag of sugar and a teaspoon of brewers yeast. You will need somewhere warmish to start your wine, which can take a couple of weeks and somewhere to store it after it is finished. You will also need a tube for siphoning it from one vessel to another – and that's all!

Sterilise everything

In all the processes of wine making, continually sterilise everything. Do not use any utensil unless it has been treated with sterilising solution. Do not use sterilising solution on metal – you can boil those.

The container that wine is mostly made in is called a demijohn. It is quite delicate and will crack if heated. Wash all your equipment; the demijohn, the cork and airlock in warmish soapy water and rinse well. Fill the demijohn with cold water and add the appropriate number of sterilising tablets. Similarly make a little more sterilising solution for the airlock, in a separate bowl.

Extracting the juice

You need to collect enough fruit / flowers / leaves to make a gallon of juice.

Collect only the best fruit, leave anything bad or rotted behind and place into muslin, tying off to make a bag. Pour in two kettles full of boiling water and mash away with a potato masher or rolling pin and leave the fruit soaking. Repeat mashing and soaking until the liquid has cooled and then squeeze the muslin bag to remove all the concentrated juice.

To this juice you can add sugar, depending on how much sugar the juice already contains. You can measure the specific gravity of the liquid and get a reasonable idea of how much sugar, but as a rule of thumb, for sweet fruit, such as grapes or strawberries I add an extra 250g of sugar, more tart wines, such as rhubarb add an extra 500g.

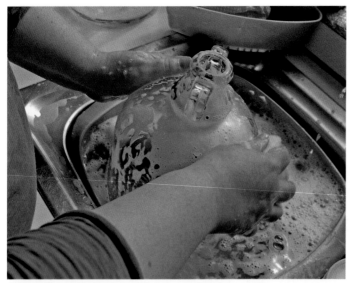

Wash all the equipment in warm soapy water and rinse well

Fill a demijohn with cold water and add the appropriate number of sterilising tablets

Add a teaspoon of brewer's yeast to the liquid. You don't need to do anything fancy just plonk it in

Putting a cork and an airlock on the demijohn

Within a day, the water in the airlock will be bubbling

Filling the jars

Sterilise all of your equipment before use and rinse the demijohn with cooled boiled water. Pour all your crushed fruit juice into the demijohn. Your syrup should first be left until just luke warm then carefully poured into the demijohn until it comes to the neck of the glass.

Give it a shake and then add a teaspoon of brewer's yeast to the liquid. You don't need to start the yeast off just pop the powder strait in the demijohn. Put a little water in the airlock and set it into position. Within a day the water in the airlock will be bubbling away as the fermentation starts. Don't worry about your juice bubbling up, or even hitting the bottom of the cork.

When the bubbling stops, around a fortnight later, transfer the wine from its brewing vessel to a second demijohn, using a siphon tube. Be careful not to include any of the yeast that has gathered in the bottom. The process of siphoning the wine is called racking. This separates the wine from the dead yeast which will spoil the flavour if left too long.

Give the wine a good shake in its new demijohn, and all the gas will come out of it. This is an important step because it allows the remains of the yeast in the wine to fall to the bottom and the liquid will gradually clear. A few days later, if you can manage to wait that long, rack the wine again back into it's original, now cleaned demijohn, this time avoiding the smaller film of yeast on the bottom.

By now you should have pretty clear wine ready to drink. Purists will say you have to bottle the wine and keep it and you can siphon this into bottles and leave it to mature. Ever ready to economise, I buy two, 2 litre bottles of lemonade from the supermarket, pour the lemonade into a jar for immediate use, leaving me with two sterile bottles ideal for storing wine. This also saves the use of sterilising chemicals.

Once racked the wine should be vigoursly shaken to get rid of CO_2

"The art is keeping everything simple"

Oak Leaf Wine

This is a really interesting, enjoyable and tasty old country wine to try. You can make this wine from young fresh leaves, larger older green leaves or even brown dried leaves. Why not try it each way – you should get a different result each time. The leaves should always be gathered direct from the tree rather than collected from the ground.

METHOD

You should collect enough leaves to fill a five litre container when reasonably well packed in. The

leaves can either be boiled for 40 minutes or if you have the patience, you can infuse the leaves in boiling water and leave for three to four days before straining them from the liquid.

Next you should re-heat the liquid add 2kgs/4lbs of sugar and stir this for 15 minutes to melt it. Allow to cool for an hour or so before adding 500g/1lb of chopped raisins and a teaspoon of brewers yeast. Transfer to a sterilised demijohn and leave somewhere warm for the fermentation process to complete which should take between two to three weeks. Rack the wine as described above before bottling.

The wine, which should have a rich varnish like colour to it is quite drinkable within three months, but if left for a year it will be enjoyed at its best.

Elderflower Champagne

You don't need demijohns for this one.

Ingredients

6 Elderflower heads
2 Lemons' juice
4 litres of water
750g (1¾lbs) sugar

METHOD

Put elderflower heads and lemons in a bucket and pour on the boiling water. Leave to soak for 24 hours, covered with a tea towel. Strain through a muslin and add sugar and lemon juice. Stir until sugar is completely dissolved and pour into two 2 Litre screw-top lemonade bottles. Leave tops slightly loose for a couple of weeks. Keep for 2 to 3 months before drinking. Serve cool on a hot summer evening.

Birch Sap Wine

The vital ingredient for this wine needs to be collected in March when the trees, which are sending the sap from their roots up to their branches, will yield enough sap. The main image at the start of this feature shows the sap being retrieved from a tree, further guidance is given in the images below. You want a tree that is at least eight inches in diameter. Two days will normally see the demijohn with enough sap. However, if you are a little early or late collecting the sap you may need to use several trees.

METHOD

You need around 4 litres of sap to make a demijohn of wine. Bring the sap to a gentle simmer and add 2kg/2.2lb of sugar 250g/½lb of chopped raisins. Simmer, stirring occasionally for 10 minutes. Allow to cool for an hour or so, then add the juice of two lemons and a teaspoon of brewers yeast. Leave to ferment for two to three weeks before racking.

Drill hole at an upward angle

Insert tube to collect sap

Once finished plug hole with earth

Country wine recipes

Raspberry wine

In the late summer we collect around a hundred pounds of raspberries from the wild. Most of this becomes wine!

Ingredients
2kg (4½lbs) raspberries
1g (2¼lbs) sugar
1 teaspoon wine yeast
1 Vitamin C tablet

The Vitamin C helps the yeast to really get going.

METHOD
Place the fruit into a muslin bag in a bucket, add a kettle of boiling water and bash away with the masher.

When you are sure you have all the juice out, allow to cool and filter it into the demijohn using another muslin bag.

Make syrup of sugar with 1 litre (1¾ pint) of boiling water and sugar, allow to cool and add to the demijohn. Top up with boiled but cooled water and add a teaspoon of yeast.

Mead

This was the Celtic drink of Marriage, and has to be kept in bottles for a long time. You need sterile bottles and corks, or plastic lids for this.

Ingredients
1.5kg (3¼lb) runny honey
Boiled water
Vitamin C tablet
Spoonful of yeast.

METHOD
Simply dissolve all the honey in water and fill to the neck of the demijohn. Add a Vitamin C tablet and yeast. The fermentation is often slow to start.

The wine is racked off as usual, and left alone for many months. Bottle when the sediment is all racked away. With each racking give a good shake. At this point the mead will taste awful. A year later and the slow chemistry will have changed the brew into something that does not taste in any way like honey.

Dandelion wine

This is great wine – lots of fun and it creates a lovely light drink for late summer. Make sure you wash the flowers thoroughly and collect them well away from where anyone might have been spraying weedkillers around.

Ingredients
Lots and Lots of dandelion flowers - keep the stems off.
Two Kettles of boiling water
Juice of two lemons
1kg (2¼lb) granulated sugar
Spoonful of yeast

METHOD
The method for this wine is exactly the same as for Raspberry wine.

Another Dandelion wine recipe

Simply mix all the ingredients but no yeast and place in stone jugs for the whole of the summer to ferment naturally. Do not use boiling water as you want the natural yeasts on the flowers do the fermenting. Also add an extra 500g (1lb) sugar.

Out of the water, into the pan (and then onto the fire)

Paul Peacock goes all hunter, gatherer on us and spends a day down by the river

"Freshwater fish taste muddy." That's what I was told anyway. But that's alright, I ate a lot of mud when I was a child. But it is not actually true and freshwater fish have been the backbone of country cooking since the Ice Age. It is said the Romans came to this country for our oysters; the Vikings for our trout and eels.

Every large house and village had a fish pond from which a large variety of fish were taken for food. Today we seem only to eat freshwater trout and freshwater salmon because these are available in the shops. The ubiquitous rainbow trout is much prized, but is an addition to British waters and the local brown trout is hardly ever seen.

But fishermen can delight in eating wonderful freshwater fish of all varieties. It is possibly the most humane way to eat fish – you see, I have a problem with the way we catch sea-fish these days.

Normally the fish we eat are collected in huge numbers and brought together in the cold hold of a boat, usually stored in ice, where they cool down and slowly suffocate over a prolonged period or are crushed to death by the weight of the catch. There is also evidence that some fish are gutted while still alive. Now I do not suggest that people should not eat fish, but it stands to reason that a fish caught on a barbless hook, causing the least discomfort, and then humanely killed with a Priest, is by far the best way to go. So for me, I have to catch my own fish, kill it and then eat it.

(A Priest is a kind of a cudgel which is used to strike the head of the fish, causing instant death – it's called a Priest because it delivers the last rites!)

Fishing reel

Be careful

Unfortunately you cannot simply go to any old river and fish it for food. Many of them are polluted, and although the water quality seems to be improving, many rivers are still heavily contaminated with heavy metals. Be sure that you know your fish are safe to eat.

Traditionally the freshwater fish eaten in this country include pike, bream, roach, tench (a bit like eating needles), perch, carp and eel. The game fish, trout, grayling and salmon were almost always taken out of the mouths of the ordinary person – being the realm of the rich, who prized them. Today however, anyone, for a price, can catch and cook their own game fish.

Killing and gutting

Fish to be eaten should be killed on the spot and preferably eaten shortly after. They are despatched

Casting

by a sharp knock between the eyes with a cudgel (the Priest). The fish should be gutted at home. Simply cut from the bottom of the fish, near the tail all the way along the centre underline of the belly. If you cut off the head and the tail, the contents of the fish are easily scooped out. If you want to keep the head, you will need to cut the gullet away from the inside. Dispose of the gullet onto newspaper, fold up and discard.

Wash the outside and the inside of the fish under running water. You then need to remove the scales by rubbing against the grain with a blunt knife, and then rewash the fish.

Perch

This is a fisherman's fish, described by Jack Hargreaves, the television presenter of *Out of Town,* as a Siamese Dragon. It is covered with stripes and has fearsome orange fins, and teeth that hold their prey in a deadly grip. They are also excellent eating – much prized by the Japanese, but not uncommon in the country kitchen.

One of the problems with cooking this fish is that it is easily over-cooked, and has a tendency to fall apart. For this reason it is often filleted and lightly fried.

Grilled perch

1 large perch, gutted and de-scaled
Salt
Freshly ground pepper
Sliced tomatoes
Whole mushrooms
Sprigs of rosemary
Olive oil

METHOD
Clean the fish completely, and season inside and out with salt and pepper. It is important the scales are completely removed. Stuff the cavity with sprigs of rosemary. Brush the fish, inside and out, with olive oil.

Place on a grill – a barbeque is an ideal way to cook this dish – for four minutes. The cooking times are important. Carefully flip the fish and add the vegetables to the grill. Cook the other side for another four minutes.

Remove the fish and allow to rest until the vegetables are finally cooked. Serve together.

Roach

These fish are the same family as carp, and make good eating. The roach features quite heavily in Chinese cooking. My friend Jon at www.waterlogmagazine.com, who just loves to eat his own catch, gave me this recipe.

Boiled roach with sorrel

For the court-bouillon
2 onions, coarsely chopped
3 cloves garlic
1 sprig thyme
1 sprig parsley
10 peppercorns
1 lemon, sliced
2 tsp salt
200ml (7fl oz) dry white wine
1 litre (1¾pt) water

And the rest…
One roach per person
A good handful of sorrel
Chopped chives and parsley
2 tablespoons of cream

METHOD
To make the court-bouillon, bring all the ingredients to the boil in a large saucepan or stockpot, simmer for 30 minutes. Strain the stock through a fine-mesh sieve, preferably lined with muslin, and use.

Poach the prepared roach in the court-bouillon or in salt and water. When cooked, arrange them on a dish and keep hot.

Boil the chopped sorrel, parsley and chives in a little salted water. Melt a piece of butter in a saucepan, add the sorrel and chopped herbs and two or three tablespoonfuls of cream.

Season, and boil, stirring well, for a minute or two and then pour the sorrel and herb sauce over the fish and serve at once.

Eel

There are a lot of old wives' tales about eels – one of them was that they still wriggle about in the frying pan – which have come from the fact that they are extraordinarily difficult to kill. They are caught with a worm on a line, or if you are a little more industrious, eel hives. An eel hive is made of willow, but you can do just as well with a weighted sack which is partly filled with straw. They are put out at midnight and collected before dawn.

You can buy live eels in specialist fishmongers – get them to gut, bone and skin the fish for you. Eel meat is quite fatty and lends itself to smoking, frying or casseroling.

Eel casserole

1 large eel, sliced into 2cm (¾inch) pieces (around 400g/⅞lb)
2 finely sliced onions
2 cloves of garlic, crushed and chopped
Bay leaf
Handful of parsley, 2 sprigs of mint
500ml (1pt) vegetable or chicken stock.

500g (1lb) potatoes, peeled and cut into 1cm (½inch) squares

METHOD
Lightly fry the onions in oil and add the garlic. Once translucent, add the fish and fry gently. As the fish browns lightly, add the chopped herbs.

Gently bring the stock to the boil. Transfer the eel and onions to a casserole and cover with stock and add the potatoes. Season as appropriate and cook at 175°C (350°F, gas 4) in the oven until the potatoes are fully soft.

Serve with freshly baked bread. You can replace one of the onions with a roughly chopped leek.

Game fish – trout and salmon

The words 'Game Fish' was really a way of the upper classes claiming these fish for themselves, and coarse fish were reserved for all the rest, because coarse men fished for them. Even the method of catching trout and salmon is shrouded in noble mystery. Fly fishing, until recently, was reserved for those who could afford to spend thousands on getting a bit of river bank to fish from.

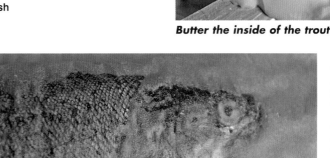
Butter the inside of the trout

Simple trout en papillote

A papillote is a paper parcel inside which food is cooked. It is made from parchment (greaseproof) paper

1 medium sized trout per person
1 tsp butter per fish
Juice of half a lemon per fish
Salt and pepper

METHOD
Make a parcel from baking paper into which you lay the washed and gutted fish. Sprinkle inside and out with salt and place the butter in the cavity. Cover the whole with lemon juice and close the parcel.

Bake at 175°C (350°F, gas 4) for 20 minutes.

Place your prepared trout in a parcel made of baking parchment

Pare away the trout flesh from the bones

Salmon
This King of fish is farmed these days, and therefore easily accessible to everyone. Wild salmon are more expensive and less pink in colour, farmed salmon are frequently fed chemicals to enhance their colour.

Simple poached salmon

1 large salmon
2 lemons, sliced
1 tbsp black pepper corns
200ml (7fl oz) white wine vinegar

METHOD
De-scale the salmon and wash inside and out.

If you do not have a fish kettle, use any large container that can take the fish and the water to cover it. Add the vinegar and other ingredients to the container and cover with boiling water.

Poach in the oven for ten minutes per pound. Check the flesh to ensure that none of it is gelatinous, and add another ten minutes if required.

Pike

This monster fish is a predator, lurking somewhere under reeds, it flashes out to eat anything from smaller fish to frogs, and when you pull them out of the water, they look you in the eye. Pike is a traditional country dish.

There are so many recipes; you can treat filleted pike like almost any other fish, particularly salmon.

Baked pike with forcemeat stuffing

For the forcemeat
100g (4oz) breadcrumbs
25g (1oz) butter
25g (1oz) suet
25g (1oz) fatty bacon
1 egg
1 onion, finely chopped
1 small handful of finely chopped parsley
Salt and pepper

And the rest ...
1 pike
25g (1oz) butter

METHOD
Mix all the forcemeat ingredients together adding the egg last, after having lightly beaten it.

I prefer to remove the head behind the gills, and the tail. Wash and cover all the surfaces with a sprinkle of salt. In the cavity break up small pieces of butter and arrange before stuffing the cavity with the forcemeat. Sew up the cavity.

Bake at 200°C (400°F, gas 6) for forty minutes. When the fish is a good brown colour, turn the oven off and leave it for another ten minutes.

Serve by slicing the fish through the body to give individual portions.

Salmon steak steamed with lemon

An eel odyssey

As **Clarissa Porter** explains eating eels has a "reputation". Bot don't worry she has plenty of traditional and tasty recipes

Smoked eel salad with dill mustard mayonnaise

If you've never tried this before, get ready for a revelation. Of course, your main problem is going to be finding smoked eels. Some fishmongers sell imported smoked eel from Scandinavia, or you may be lucky to live near to a smokery. My local fishmonger doesn't stock the imported eels any more, he says they are too expensive for his customers. This would make an elegant starter, or a light supper.

Serves 4-6

Smoked eel pieces, about 110g (4oz) to 175g (6oz) per person
Baby salad leaves
A few walnuts
A few cubes of white bread doused in olive oil and fried to make croutons

For the mayonnaise
Bunch of dill, finely chopped
1tbsp French mustard
2 egg yolks
250ml (9fl oz) of olive oil
2tbsp white wine vinegar

METHOD
First make the mayonnaise, with a whisk or in a blender, whisk the egg yolks and add the olive oil drip by drip until the sauce begins to thicken. Add the wine vinegar, then the mustard and finely chopped dill. If necessary, thin with a little cream. Then arrange a few eel slices on to the baby leaves, drizzle on the mayonnaise and scatter a few croutons, don't over do the croutons, the eels are such a subtle taste they shouldn't be smothered by another taste.

When I told my friends I would be cooking some traditional eel recipes, they all reacted with the same screwed-up noses and "yuk." Very few foods produce such a strong reaction. Why is that I wonder? And though the eel is a true delicacy, I have even met fishmongers that have never tasted them. But, love them or loathe them they are part of our cooking heritage.

This extraordinary fish has been celebrated throughout recorded culinary history, from the Greeks and Romans, down to today. It has even given its name to places such as the Isle of Ely, and Eel Pie Island. Most people associate only one dish with eels, and that is of course jellied eels, and although my friends recoiled in distaste at the very idea of eating jellied eels, none had actually tried them. Which is a sorry state of affairs! So I am on a mission to promote The Appreciation of the Eel.

Firstly, an eel's life story. An extraordinary story that covers thousands of miles, and to this day is not completely documented. No one has yet succeeded in filming a complete lifecycle of an eel. Until quite recently people thought they came magically from the earth, or that they were a type of earthworm. Isaak Walton records in his book "The Compleat Angler," published in 1653, that some people believe they are formed from dew drops in the months of May and June, the Sun's heat turning the drops into eels!

The reality is just as strange. European eels spawn their young in the Sargasso Sea, near Bermuda. A female eel can produce 10 million larvae! The tiny transparent larvae drift on ocean currents for up to three years and over 3,000 miles till they reach our shores. When they arrive, they develop into tiny transparent 'Glass Eels'. When they enter freshwater, they become Elvers, and change colour and darken. As they grow, some travel upstream, and some migrate up and downstream. The further up river they go the more they change colour to brown or 'gold'. The females are more likely to migrate upstream, the males preferring to live in coastal areas. The females can live upstream for as long as 16 years. They can travel short distances over land, and burrow through sand for up to 30 miles! This explains how you can find eels in lakes and ponds far away from rivers. At some point in their lives, they feel the need to return to the sea, usually at this time of the year, September and October, when the sea is wild and stormy. They change colour again to a bluey silvery black, and begin the long swim back to the Sargasso Sea, where they spawn and die.

What an extraordinary story! Sadly, in the last 10 years, eel stocks have declined dramatically. This is nothing to do with over-fishing. It appears that a parasite is attacking the Eels, and stocks are perhaps 10 per cent of what they were in 1990. This means that there has been a dramatic increase in the price you'll be paying at the fishmongers. Eels are currently more expensive, kilo for kilo, than sea bass.

If you've never tasted eel, I can't recommend it enough. Eel has the firm texture of a prawn, and the light taste of plaice. Smoked eel is a true delicacy, but you'll have to search for it! I bought my eels at the Estuary Fish Merchants in Leigh on Sea in Essex. A real old-time enterprise situated in Cockle Shed Row. They have their own smokery and are happy to let you taste before you buy. Eels are sold live, so I recommend you ask the fishmonger to kill them for you! And clean and gut them, and remove the heads and skin. But please do try Eels, I guarantee you will be surprised and converted.

All the following recipes are traditional and very British. Eel pie and mash shops used to be a familiar sight around the country, particularly in London. Now they have all but disappeared, I know of two still operating, Goddards in Greenwich, and Manze in Peckham. Visiting these two establishments is an experience to be grabbed while you still can, they are remnants of a once thriving trade. •

Eel pie

There are many variations to this essentially traditional dish. You can adapt it to your taste. A proper filling meal, straight out of the pages of Dickens or Shakespeare.

Serves 4-6

750g (1½lb) – 1kg (2lb) eels, skinned, Boned and sliced
25g (1oz) flour
2 slices of streaky bacon, chopped
1tbsp parsley, chopped
Nutmeg
Salt and pepper
3 hard boiled eggs, quartered
275ml (9fl oz) milk
225g (8oz) puff pastry (ready made)
1 egg, beaten

METHOD

Toss the eel pieces in flour seasoned with salt and pepper. Place the eel pieces in a greased baking tray and cover with greaseproof paper or foil and bake in an oven heated to 190°C (375°F, gas 5) for about 20 minutes. Remove from the oven. Grease a pie dish and place the eels and the bacon in the dish, then arrange the quartered hard-boiled eggs among the eel pieces. Season with pepper and salt and a few scrapes of nutmeg. Scatter parsley and pour over the milk. Roll out the puff pastry and cover the pie dish. Decorate the pastry with left over pieces and glaze with the egg yolk. Return to the oven and bake for 20 to 25 minutes until the pastry has risen and is golden brown. Serve with mashed potatoes (if you like you can add chopped spring onions to the mash), and mushy peas.

"Eel has the firm texture of a prawn, and the light taste of plaice"

Isaak Walton's roast eel

"The Compleat Angler" published in 1653 has a chapter devoted to eels. This is the recipe from that chapter, only slightly adapted for 2006. I suggest you try and stick as much to the original recipe as possible, and I promise you this is a really excellent dish. They certainly knew how to cook their fish 350 years ago! What an adventure it must have been to have travelled with Mr Walton. This is a truly simple but magnificent dish, shut your eyes and be transported back 350 years to the banks of the Thames alongside Isaak Walton.

1 eel (depending on the size, would serve 2 or 3 people)
110g (3½oz) butter
Nutmeg
Pepper
Salt
'Sweet herbs' such as marjoram, oregano, tarragon, parsley
Spinach leaves
2 anchovy fillets

ISAAK WALTON'S METHOD
Prepare your eel, remove the head. Wash the eel in water and salt. Then pull off the skin down to near the tail, but don't completely remove it. Now gut the eel, but don't wash it any more. Make 3 or 4 scotches (slices, cuts, slashes) in the side of the eel. Into those scotches and into the belly cavity put the sweet herbs, the anchovy and a little nutmeg cut very small and mixed with butter and salt. Then you pull the skin back over the eel and tie it where the head was. Tie it tight. Then Isaak would have tied the eel to a spit and roasted it over an open fire, basting with water and salt till the skin burst. Then after a final basting with butter, the eel would be served with the juices as its own sauce.

CLARISSA PORTER'S METHOD
Remove the skin and guts from the eel, cut into pieces about 4 inches long. Place some spinach leaves on some foil and lay the eel pieces on top. Make a few slashes in the side of the eel. Mix together the nutmeg, herbs, butter, pepper, salt and anchovies chopped, and stuff inside the eel and into the cuts in the body. Place more spinach leaves on top of the fish, make a parcel of the foil and bake for about 30 minutes in a moderate oven, or for slightly less time on a barbecue. Serve with sliced boiled potatoes.

"Eels are sold live, so ask the fishmonger to kill them for you"

Jellied eels

You really must try jellied eels. They are deliciously light and cool with a subtle taste. Tradition, history, its all there on your plate!

Serves 4-6

900g (2lb) eels, skinned and cut into pieces about 1 inch long
Juice of one lemon
6 peppercorns
1 small onion, quartered
Parsley
Bleaf

METHOD
Place the eels in a pan of warm water, add all the other ingredients except the parsley, bring to the boil and simmer for about 30 minutes. Then lift out the eel pieces. Skim off any froth from the liquid with a piece of stale bread. Strain the liquid, and then strain again. Place the pieces of eel in a serving bowl and pour in the now cool liquid. Stir in the chopped parsley. Serve, with brown bread and maybe salad leaves.

Barbequed sea bass

This is about as simple as you can get with cooked fish, and is therefore ideal for the beach or an impromptu feast!

1 medium fish per person. No need to remove scales
Olive oil
Garlic clove, thinly sliced

METHOD
Score the sides of the fish a few times and wash in clean water to remove any loose scales.

Brush the fish and the grill with oil and scatter over the sliced garlic. Place on the barbeque and cook for a few minutes on each side. Time will vary depending on barbeque heat, but 2-3 minutes will normally suffice.

Barbequed fish

Dave Costar asks: Can anything be better than a family outing to the beach on a summer's day, catching a few fish then cooking them on a barbeque?

We were very lucky on a recent trip to have a superb catch of three sea bass, together with the usual glut of mackerel! Any well-prepared fisherman/chef always sets off with the anticipation of a successful trip, and on this one we carried a few essentials to help with the preparation. A little olive oil, some herbs, tomatoes, garlic and a few lemons and chillies.

Although we intended to make our BBQ using driftwood found on the beach, we eventually needed to use bought charcoal, as we had picked what must have been the cleanest beach around, devoid of such useful items as driftwood!

Obviously the fish you catch will not be ready-prepared, however the task is really not difficult. Mackerel do not need to be scaled, although sea bass sometimes do, depending on the recipe.

To remove the scales, hold the tail of the fish and scrape toward the head with the back of a knife. The scales will flick off easily, leaving a silvery smooth skin. To gut the fish, cut the belly from the anal vent towards the front, between the two pectoral fins. Open the flaps and remove the insides. Wash out cavity with clean water.

I hope you like these recipes, we certainly did! ●

Sea bass Provencale

I adapted this recipe from a dish I had in Southern France. That one was made with cod, but sea bass probably works even better. It is a simple dish, designed to enhance the delicate flavour of the fish.

1 medium fish per person
½ green pepper, thinly sliced
½ red pepper, thinly sliced
6 tomatoes, chopped
Dry white wine, ½ glass
½ clove garlic, sliced
Dried herbs to season

METHOD

Scale and clean the fish, then place onto a piece of foil large enough to fully wrap the fish. Scatter the sliced peppers and tomatoes around the fish, and pour over the white wine. Sprinkle with herbs and sliced garlic then wrap, folding the foil into a seal on the top.

Place on a heated barbeque and cook for 10 minutes on each side. Because the fish is protected by the foil, this can be started off when the barbeque is still too hot for cooking fish 'au natural'.

Serve in the foil with a simple salad and sliced French bread. The remainder of the white wine provides an excellent accompaniment!

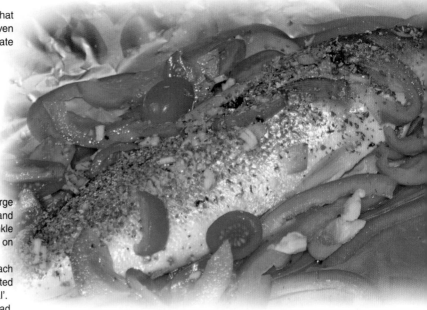

Spicy sea bass

This addition of chilli pepper adds a nice tang to the fish, without overwhelming its flavour.

1 medium fish per person
6 tomatoes, chopped
2 chilli peppers, finely chopped
Olive oil

METHOD

Scale and clean the fish, then stuff the cavity with the chopped tomatoes and chilies. Place onto a piece of foil large enough to fully wrap the fish and drizzle with olive oil.

Any remaining tomatoes and chilies can be placed around the fish. Wrap the fish, folding the foil into a seal and cook for 10 minutes on each side.

Serve in the foil with salad, bread and wine.

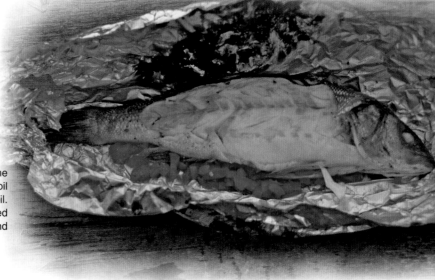

Mackerel stuffed with lemon slices

Fresh mackerel is a wonderful fish, and when just caught is a world away from those sourced from the local supermarket. Adding lemon slices to the fish helps to keep it really moist, despite the heat from the barbeque.

1 mackerel per person
Lemon, thinly sliced, about 2 slices per fish
Olive oil

METHOD

Place 2 lemon slices into each fish. Brush the fish and the grill with oil. Place on the barbeque and cook for a few minutes on each side.

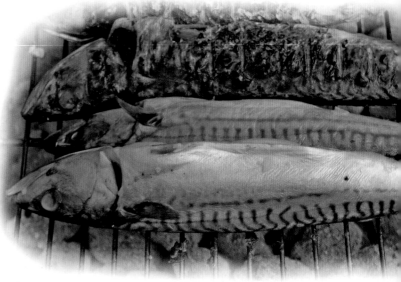

Mussels

The mussels and cockles, scallops, razors, clams and oysters that come from UK waters are simply the best in the world. They are fished and sent abroad In huge quantities. In particular, our mussel beds are beyond compare, It Is a complete shame that we do not eat them more often in this country.

To begin with there are some rules about preparing molluscs for eating. When you collect them they should be eaten as soon as possible. Any open shells should be discarded if, once tapped on the table, they remain so. Some molluscs hold themselves to rocks with strands of protein called beards, which should be pulled away to stop them spoiling the dish.

● Make sure that the sea water they are collected from is clean and there are no sewage outfalls nearby.
● Scrub the shells in running water.
● Once cooked, any shell that remains closed should be discarded.

Marinated Mussels

This dish can be adapted, replacing mussels with anything available. The sauce tastes like concentrated sea-side, and whereas we use wine in this recipe, you could go mad and use brandy.

Ingredients

An onion, large and finely chopped
30g (1oz) butter
Garlic, 2 to 3 cloves, finely crushed
15g (½oz) flour
Half a bottle of white wine
300ml (½pint) double cream
800g (1¾lbs) mussels
Chopped parsley

METHOD

First melt the butter in a steep sided pan and sweat off the onions and garlic until they are translucent, after which you sprinkle the flour into the butter mix to thicken. Stir well to avoid lumps, and continue to cook for another three minutes.

Slowly add the wine, stirring all the time. Continue to stir until the sauce is beginning to thicken.

Add the mussels to the sauce, and shake the pan well to settle the contents. Immediately cover with a lid and turn up the heat; the wine is now steaming the mussels, and this should take between 12 and 15 minutes to complete. Check the dish and stir every few minutes, replacing the lid each time.

When all the shells are open, turn down the heat and slowly add the cream, stirring and allowing the sauce to thicken. Finally season and add a generous amount of parsley.

Serve with freshly baked bread.

The Glorious 12th

August plays host to the most well-known day on the gaming calendar

Tradition and economics play a huge role in this wonderfully British day, when the grouse shooting season commences.

Red Grouse breed unmolested on the heather moors of northern Britain before hunters are free to organise their shooting parties on that fateful (if you're a grouse) day, one that often sees guns heading up from the capital for the weekend to bag a brace or two for expensive London restaurants.

And that's where economics come into the equation. While in today's society there are increasing numbers who campaign against traditional British pastimes, statistics show that August 12th injects more than £12 million into the countryside, meaning the income from grouse shooting-related tourism is crucial to the prosperity of thousands of local businesses, ranging from catering companies to game dealers, from hotels and pubs to agricultural contractors and small farms.

Sautéed grouse breasts

Serves 2

2 grouse breasts
Fresh garlic
Black pepper
7-8 juniper berries
Paprika
Sage
Thyme
Flour
450ml (16fl oz) brandy
Oil:butter (50:50) for frying

METHOD

Soak breasts in seasoned flour. Crush the juniper berries and use with other seasonings. Brown the garlic in oil and butter and set aside. Brown the breasts and add 225ml (7½fl oz) of brandy, preheated. Flame the breasts (light the brandy and allow to burn while stirring constantly), being careful of the flames. Cover the skillet and allow the breasts to simmer until done. Do not overcook.

Just before removing meat, add another 2-3 tbsp of chopped garlic and another juniper berry or two, and sauté lightly. Then add more brandy (up to 225ml) and flame as before. Remove breasts to plate. Degrease the pan if necessary, and boil the pot liquor to reduce. Thicken with seasoned flour, correct the seasoning, and serve with boiled rice to which sautéed mushrooms have been added.

Grouse breast with ham sauce

Serves 2

2 grouse breasts
1 tsp celery salt
50g (2oz) butter
6 green onions, chopped
100g (4oz) ham, diced
225ml (7½fl oz) single cream
120ml (4fl oz) chicken stock
2 tbsp sherry wine
1 tbsp chopped parsley
Salt
Pepper

METHOD

Rub grouse breasts with celery salt, salt, and pepper. Fry in butter for 35 minutes, or until done. Add green onions, ham, cream, and broth. Cook slowly for 15 minutes. If too thin, add a little flour mixed with water. Add sherry and parsley. Serve each breast on toast and top with sauce.

Wild Fruits

Harvest them now; the time is ripe

Blackberries

Later summer/autumn brings a good number of particularly useful items to the forefront of the wild food collector's basket, one of the most succulent being the blackberry.

Indeed, no country kitchen would be complete at this time of year without a blackberry and apple pie cooling on the side. As Delia Smith says, they are "best of all made with wild brambles, which seem to have twice as much flavour as the cultivated kind."

Battling with prickles to bring home a brimming basket takes you back to your childhood, and few afternoon activities on a bright autumn day can provide you with quite the same satisfaction.

The facts

Rubus is a genus of 250 or more species growing as both deciduous and evergreen shrubs and climbers, and is often bristly or prickly. Blackberries or brambles, *R. fruticosus* and their raspberry cousins, *R. ideaus*, are cultivated for their fruits, but plenty of the former are to be found growing almost anywhere and everywhere in the wild. It is believed that there are some 400 micro-species in Britain and they have been a popular source of food for centuries. In ancient times, blackberries were symbols of healing, protection and money. Blackberry leaves, when moistened, were once used as a cure for scalds.

They are a great source of vitamins and minerals, including, vitamin A, vitamin C, calcium, folate, magnesium and iron.

Picking blackberries

The berries ripen from the tips of the stalks, usually sometime in August. The big, fat ones right at the tip are the sweetest and are probably best eaten raw, but the rest of the crop will continue ripening until October and are excellent for making jams and pies, though they may need to be cooked with other fruits and with some added sweetening.

Great wines to accompany blackberries

Colombard

Grenache Rose

Cabernet Sauvignon

Sauternes

Vouvray

Moscato D-Asti

Auslesen

Picking and cultivating wild blackberries

The best blackberries have a habit of growing alongside stinging nettles and you tend to be picking the fruit when the nettles are at their largest – sometimes 2 Meters tall! Dress appropriately and take a good stick, such as a broom stick, which can be an invaluable tool for reaching the best fruits. Hammer a nail in one end and you can pull the fruits that are out of reach into easy picking territory.

If you find a particularly tasty blackberry that you would like to cultivate for your garden you don't need to use rooting powders to grow cuttings. Simply peg down the tips of some of the blackberry shoots with some strong wire, such as fencing wire. This is called layering and will encourage the tips to root. Shoots layered at this time of year would be ready for transplanting early in spring. Alternatively, tips layered in spring can be transplanted in the autumn.

This garden hedge is only four years old and the specially selected and layered blackberries are only two years old. The hedge which has a good old Bramley apple tree at one end is about 15 foot long and also contains Kent cob nuts grown from wild nuts and damsons also grown from the wild. Other fruits growing in this little hedge include crab apples and apricots. Oh, and wild garlic grows under Bramley trees in the spring.

Blackberry and apple pie

Use a sweetened shortcrust pastry for a blackberry and apple pie. Equal proportions of plain flour and fat – a mix of lard and baking margarine is best – rubbed together until the mixture is crumbly. Sprinkle a tablespoonful of sugar over and add water by the tablespoon and continue mixing and cutting with a broad-bladed knife until the pastry lump leaves the bowl clean.

Wrap it in clingfilm or foil and put it away in the fridge for half-an-hour or so.

When the pastry is ready, take just enough to cover the flat rim of the pie dish, roll that out on a lightly floured board and set it around the rim, which should be brushed with cold water to make the pastry stick.

Core, peel and slice the apples into the dish, add the blackberries all over – the proportions between the two are merely a matter of taste and availability – and sprinkle a few tablespoons of sugar over the top.

Dampen the strip of pastry around the rim of the dish, roll out the rest of the pastry for the lid and cover the pie, trimming the edges neatly and crimp or flute them as you choose. Make a couple of holes in the centre of the pie to let out the steam and brush it all over with cold milk and a dusting of caster sugar.

Bake it at 220°C (Gas 7) for 10 minutes and then reduce the heat to 190°C (Gas 5) for another 25 minutes or so. You can test to see whether the apples are cooked sufficiently with a skewer, but generally when the pastry is nicely browned they will be done perfectly, too.

Serve with as much cream as you think you can get away with.

Chilled blackberry meringue

Serves 8-10

Ingredients
570ml (1pint) double cream
50g (2oz) light muscovado sugar
2 tbsp cocoa
4 meringue nests
450g (1lb) blackberries
Icing sugar, for dusting

METHOD

Whip the cream until it just holds its shape, then stir in the sugar and sift in the cocoa.

Break up the meringue nests into small pieces and lightly mash the blackberries with a fork. Stir both lightly into the cream.

Line a loaf tin with cling film. Spoon in the dessert mixture, pressing it into the corners, gently smooth the top. Cover and freeze until firm, about 4 hours.

About an hour before serving, transfer the dessert from the freezer to the fridge. When ready to serve, turn out on to a flat serving plate, dust the top with sifted icing sugar and scatter blackberries over the top. Chill until ready to serve.

Hazelnuts

Hazelnuts are also well worth the collector's time and trouble. The bushes grow around and among larger woodland and frequently in hedgerows. The nuts ripen around the middle of September and it's a race, then, between birds, squirrels and ourselves to see who is going to get the lion's share. As a rule, hazel bushes are not terribly high, the branches are pliable and easily pulled down with a walking stick and the nuts come away quite easily.

They shouldn't be gathered green, of course, since they won't ripen off the bush. Check the colour of the shells of any fallen nuts you are able to find – if these are very dark or a greyish brown then the kernels inside will almost certainly be withered or turned to dust.

Eaten whole in front of the fire on a chilly autumn evening or whenever you fancy, really, these nuts are not only exceedingly tasty but also extremely good for you. One expert says that, weight for weight, they contain 50 per cent

more protein, seven times more fat and five times more carbohydrate than hens' eggs.

They can also be eaten chopped, or ground and can be added to biscuits, cakes, and other desserts, or used in salads or to make a savory butter to flavor entrées and side dishes. Like many nuts, roasting hazelnuts brings out their flavor. After roasting, hazelnuts should be rubbed in a cloth while still hot to remove their skins.

The nuts should be kept in their shells if you're not going to use them right away. The oil in shelled hazelnuts can become rancid quickly and so they should be used within a week, refrigerated for up to six months, or frozen for up to one year. For long-term storage, it's best to buy unshelled nuts.

Cheesecake

Finely chopped or crushed and added to sweet oat biscuits they are splendid as the foundation of a cheesecake. For an average sort of size, take four ounces of the biscuits and two ounces of nuts. Toast the nuts first to a golden brown in

Blackberry trifle

Serves 2

Ingredients
30g (1oz) Amaretti biscuits
Knob of butter
1 tbsp soft brown sugar
Pinch of ground cinnamon
Pinch of mixed spice
2 tsp dark rum (or any other alcohol of your choice)
1 orange, peeled and segmented
2 tbsp double cream, whipped
Handful of blackberries

METHOD

Place the Amaretti biscuits, butter, sugar, cinnamon and spice into a food processor and blend to form a crumb-like mixture.

Spoon some of the mixture into the base of a tall serving glass or dish.

Sprinkle over the rum (or alcohol) and then scatter the orange segments on top.

Add a layer of whipped cream before another layer of orange segments and biscuit mixture.

Add more whipped cream to the glass.

Finish with a layer of blackberries and a sprig of mint.

Hazelnut Pesto

75g (3oz) hazelnuts
2 cloves peeled garlic
1 tsp salt
2 large handfuls of fresh parsley, washed and dried
100ml (3½ fl oz) extra virgin olive oil

Chop the garlic and pound it with the parsley, hazelnuts and salt until smooth. You can use a pestle and mortar, food processor or blender. While blending, trickle the oil in, a little at a time, until you have a thick paste.

a hot oven – this takes about five minutes, but they need checking and might take a little longer.

Let them cool, then chop them into small pieces. Crush the biscuits fairly lightly with a rolling pin and mix them with the nuts and 30g of melted butter. Pack the mixture into the bottom of the cheesecake tin – you'll find it's a vast improvement on the standard base, which is usually biscuit only.

Dave Costar suggests a couple of beverages we can make for virtually nothing.

Blackberry cordial

The hedgerows are laden with these succulent black fruit, so why not pick enough for a few batches of this tasty cordial. This recipe is best if large ripe juicy berries are used.

600g (1¼lb) blackberries
100g (3½oz) sugar
2 tsp cinnamon pieces
2 tsp whole cloves

METHOD
Mash the fruit, and strain through a sieve, pressing the fruit with the back of a spoon to extract as much juice as possible. Add the liquid to a saucepan and to every 300ml (½pint) of liquid, add 100g (3½oz) of sugar. Add the cloves and cinnamon. Bring to the boil and simmer for 20-25 minutes, stirring regularly as the liquid reduces and thickens. Strain through a sieve to remove the spice pieces, and pour into clean sterilized bottles. Store in the refrigerator.

To Serve
Dilute as required in glasses of iced sparkling water. Also makes great ice lollies!

Bramble jelly

900g (2lb) blackberries
300ml (½pint) water
Juice of 1 lemon
900g (2lb) caster sugar

Put the fruit, water and lemon juice into a large saucepan. Cover and cook for 15 to 30 minutes or until the fruit is very soft. Drain overnight through a jelly bag

Measure the juice and add 450g (1lb) sugar for every 600ml (1 pint) juice. Place both in a large heavy-based pan and bring the mixture slowly to the boil, stirring all the time until the sugar has dissolved. Boil rapidly until the jelly registers 105°C, (220°F) or test for setting by putting a small amount on to a cold saucer. (Chill for 3 minutes, then push the mixture with your finger; if the surface wrinkles, it is ready). Cool for 10 minutes. Skim off any scum and pour the jelly into warmed, sterilised jars. Cover and seal while the jelly is still hot and label when the jars are cold. Makes 900g (2lb).

Blackberry coulis

Blackberries
Sugar
Water

Place the blackberries into a pan with just enough water to cover the berries and sugar to taste. Cook until soft, then allow to cool for about 15 minutes. Puree in a food processor until smooth and pass through a sieve to remove the seeds. Pour straight over ice-cream, pancakes, meringue etc or place into warmed, sterilised jars to store until needed.

Blackberry tea

While picking the ingredients for the blackberry cordial, why not try picking a few handfuls of blackberry leaves and try this light, refreshing tea. Pick the very young, fresh, light green leaves which are plentiful, even at the end of the season. Dry the leaves on a low heat in the oven and when fully dry, finely crush them. Store the crushed leaves in an airtight container. When required, place 2 teaspoons of crushed leaves per cup into a teapot, and top up with boiling water. Leave to steep for 5-10 minutes, and then strain through a tea strainer into glasses or cups.

Blackberry vinegar

450g (1lb) blackberries
600ml (1 pint) white wine vinegar
450g (1lb) sugar

Place the fruit and vinegar in a covered bowl and leave to steep for 3-5 days, stirring occasionally. Strain the liquid and measure it. Add 450g (1lb) of sugar for every 600ml (1 pint) of juice and heat in a pan, stirring until the sugar dissolves, then bring to the boil. Pour into bottles and cover when cool. Use for salad dressings or as a flavouring in sauces and desserts. Historically this was used as a cough remedy.

In a Nutshell

Nutrition in a nutshell –
that's what Kentish
cobnuts offer. What's more,
they're traditonal, regional and
fresh from the tree right now,
says *Lindsay Harriss*

Our Victorian ancestors knew a thing or two. They certainly knew what a Kentish cobnut was – a question that might leave some of us 'umming' and 'aahing'. Quite simply, it's a type of hazelnut, now growing wild in the countryside which was cultivated mainly on the Greensand Ridge, between Sevenoaks, Maidstone and Charing. Unlike many other nuts, which are dried, cobnuts are sold as fresh fruit. The season is short – harvesting begins in mid to late August and runs to the end of October – but in cool, dry conditions, they can be kept fresh for many months.

The Victorians enjoyed them so much they found ingenious ways of preserving their supplies, in an era before refrigeration. A favourite method was to put the nuts on the cellar floor and scatter them with salt or, squirrel-like, cottage gardeners would place the cobnuts in tin boxes and bury them in the garden, digging them up when required. However, tins were often forgotten and some have recently been unearthed like buried treasure, complete with their booty of stored nuts, although probably not so edible after 100 years in the ground! Our storage solutions are a little easier and popping an open-topped container of Kentish Cobnuts in the fridge, should do the trick.

Here we go gathering nuts...

Grown in plantations known as Platts, the Kentish Cobnut season traditionally began on 20th August, St Philbert's Day, and cultivated hazelnuts are sometimes known as filberts. Nuts harvested early in the season are green and juicy and by the end of October their shells are brown and they are ripe and full-flavoured. Enjoy them as they are, lightly roasted with a little salt, or added to your favourite nutty recipe.

And banish any feelings of guilt – they are rich in Vitamin E and Calcium, Vitamins B1 and B6, plus they are also a good source of protein and fibre.

Harvesting nuts was a family occasion and, until the First World War, many village schools would close on Holy Cross Day, 14th September, when the day was spent gathering nuts. Various folklores grew up around the tradition, and it was thought to be dangerous to go 'nutting' on Sunday, as it was said you were likely to encounter the Devil, holding the branches of the trees down for nut pickers.

Although cultivated hazelnuts are thought to have been grown in Britain since at least the 16th Century, they really came into their own in the 19th Century, as the Victorians were quite 'nutty' about Kentish cobnuts. And by 1913 there were, reportedly, about 7000 acres of Kentish Cobnut trees. Sadly, by the 1980s this had sunk to a low of less than 250 acres, as many Platts were grubbed out and replaced by more lucrative crops. In 1990, the Kentish Cobnuts Association was established, and with the assistance of grants from The Countryside Stewardship Scheme, new cobnut trees have now been planted.

Reversing the trend

Karin and Barry Craddock planted 600 new cobnut trees seven years ago, on their land in Rolvenden. They studied old diagrams of Kentish cobnut platts and discovered that the trees were planted in a traditional 'Quintox Pattern' – a series of diagonal lines – and decided to maintain this tradition in their own platt. It takes some time for the trees to bear a decent crop, but Karin reports that this year looks like their first good harvest, and they hope to market the nuts from their website at www.farnellfarm.co.uk.

John Cannon, Chairman of the Kentish Cobnuts Association, has been growing cobnuts for about 25 years, with some 15 different varieties on his 30 acres of land in Roughway, near Tonbridge. Although the oldest part of his platt dates back 150 years, over the last 10 years he has been busily planting and his newest trees are only two years old. Varieties of Kentish cobnuts include the impressively named Merveille de Bollwiller, Gunslebert, Ennis, and the eponymous Kentish Cob which, although the name of a variety, also lends its title to the generic term for all Kentish cobnuts. Interestingly, cobnut trees are largely self-sterile, which means that they need to be fertilised by pollen from another variety of cobnut, or from a wild hazel. So, enthusiasts must plant two different, compatible varieties, or have nearby wild hazels to pollinate their trees.

Green Nuts

Growing mainly on the edge of a designated Area of Outstanding Natural Beauty, Kentish cobnuts play a valuable role in sustaining local flora and fauna, and have many environmental benefits. Meg Game, who grows them in Ightham, near Sevenoaks, described how dormice, an endangered species, love to live in the platts. They are seldom seen but tell-tale signs – like little holes nibbled in the nuts or small, round nests of grass – give away their presence. As dormice cause little damage to the crop they are welcome visitors. Red Squirrels, another endangered species, also benefits from the Kentish cobnut, as many growers sell part of their crop to conservationists who use it to feed this rare animal in areas where it still survives. According to one such conservationist in Scotland, when given the choice, the rather discerning Red Squirrels preferred the Kentish cobnuts to Italian hazelnuts.

Brian Rudd, who has been growing them in Ightham for 18 years, has 500 trees which, like most growers, he prunes to chest height. Without pruning, they can grow up to 20 or 30 feet, making them more difficult to harvest. However, he leaves one area of his platt untrimmed, as it plays host to an array of flora, with an abundant carpet of bluebells and some wild orchids. Wood Anemones, Red Campion, Speedwell and Wood Sorrel, can also be found growing in cobnut platts. The local fauna certainly find this a welcoming habitat, with deer, rabbits, foxes and birds, such as the Nuthatch, making use of the natural sanctuary. The Grey Squirrels, who always seem to know just when the cobnuts are ripe, are less welcome. Another unwelcome thief is the badger. Karin Craddock explained: "Badgers from the surrounding woodland climb up the trees for the nuts and break the branches. We've had to fence in the trees to protect them."

Growing on a bed of Kentish Ragstone, the trees thrive on relatively poor, stony soil, making use of land which apple trees, another popular crop in the area, may shun. The cobnuts are relatively resistant to disease so, with little need for spraying, most are grown naturally; in fact, some crops are organic.

Allens Farm, in Plaxtol, near Sevenoaks, is a family-run farm which has achieved full organic status, validated by The Organic Farmers and Growers Organisation, as well as receiving accolades from celebrity chef, Rick Stein. Jill Webb, of the farm, told how her family has been growing cobnuts for three generations and how her wish to maintain this heritage, plus her love of growing 'a Kentish product in Kent', inspires her to continue. The family also grow cherries and damsons and keep Southdown Sheep, which roam free in the platt, helping to maintain the trees by nibbling the buds from their bases which, if allowed to grow, would become a mass of unruly wands.

However, these wands also have their uses. Alexander Hunt, Secretary of the Kentish Cobnuts Association and long-time resident of the appropriately-named village of St Mary's Platt, explained how unwanted wands can be used as bean-poles, or even walking sticks. Also, he has been talking to Truffle UK, a company based in Dorset, about growing truffles on the roots of some of the trees. Apparently, truffle spores grow best on the roots of younger trees, which could certainly benefit growers like Alexander, who has planted half an acre of new trees in recent years. Truffles are a valuable, sought-after culinary delicacy, which could be a boon for Kentish cobnut growers, who often maintain the platts for the love of it, rather than for any economic reward. Mind you, the market for cobnuts is wide and varied – one of Alexander Hunt's customers even purchases his larger nut clusters, dips them in wax and turns them into decorations which are used to grace the tables of fine restaurants in the Netherlands!

Brian Rudd sells his Kentish cobnuts per five kilo box, mainly by mail order, to a dedicated following of customers. In fact, one hasn't missed a harvest in the last 16 years. "We get customers from all over the country – Scotland to Penzance," says Brian. So, no need to lose out if you don't live in Kent, and you might find a grower near you, as there are some commercial producers in other counties too. If you prefer to pick your own, visit Tom Maynard's farm in Ticehurst, East Sussex, where pick-your-own apples and plums are also available during the Kentish cobnut season. Alternatively, you can find them in supermarkets such as Waitrose and Morrisons, buy them at local Farmers' Markets, or go direct to the growers, details of whom can be obtained from the Kentish Cobnuts Association. ●

The Kentish Cobnuts Association,
Apple Trees, Comp Lane, St Mary's Platt, Sevenoaks, Kent, TN15 8NR. Tel: 01732 882734; e-mail: info@kentishcobnutsassociation.co.uk; or visit www.kentishcobnutsassociation.co.uk

Kentish cobnut, Stilton & apple salad

A wonderful way to enjoy Kentish cobnuts straight from the trees, as fresh green fruit or, if preferred, lightly roasted for a rich nutty flavour.

1 apple, cored and thinly sliced
2 sticks of celery, thinly sliced
A bag of mixed salad leaves
1 red onion, thinly sliced into rings
115g (4oz) Kentish cobnuts, roughly chopped (or lightly roasted)
170g (6oz) of Stilton, crumbled

For the salad dressing
1 tbsp honey
3 tbsp cider vinegar
3 tbsp hazelnut oil
A pinch of salt
A twist of freshly ground black pepper

METHOD
Place the mixed salad leaves, sliced celery and red onion in a large bowl and mix together. Scatter the apple slices and crumbled Stilton on top. Place all the salad dressing ingredients in a jam jar and shake together vigorously. Drizzle the dressing over the salad and sprinkle the Kentish cobnuts on top. Serve immediately.

Kentish cobnut & blackberry meringue gateau

The 'mellow fruitfulness' of autumn, combined in a deliciously indulgent dessert.

3 egg whites
175g (6oz) caster sugar
50g (2oz) Kentish cobnuts, lightly toasted and finely chopped
300ml (½ pint) double cream
350g (12oz) blackberries
A further handful of chopped roasted Kentish cobnuts, for scattering
A little icing sugar for dusting

METHOD

Draw a 20cm (8in) circle on two pieces of baking paper, then place each one, drawing side down, on a separate baking tray. Pre-heat the oven to 140°C (275°F, gas 1). Place the egg whites in a bowl and whisk until they become very stiff. Add the caster sugar a little at a time, whisking between additions, until all the sugar is added and the mixture is shiny. Carefully fold in the 50g (2oz) finely chopped cobnuts. Spread the mixture, in equal quantities, onto the two baking trays, using the drawn circles as a guideline to create two circles of meringue. Make soft swirls and peaks on the top of one of the meringues.

Place the baking trays in the oven and bake for a long time (2-3 hours) until the meringues are dry. When cooked, turn the heat off and leave the meringues to cool in the oven. When cool, take them out and peel off the baking paper. Place the smooth-surfaced meringue on a large plate. Whip the cream until it holds soft peaks and spread onto the smooth-surfaced meringue. Position the blackberries on top of the cream and carefully place the other meringue circle, peaked side up, on top of the fruit. Scatter the remaining chopped cobnuts over the top of the gateau and dust with icing sugar. Serve immediately.

Pumpkin & Kentish cobnut teabread

Give yourself a Halloween treat… the trick is to keep this scrumptious seasonal teabread all to yourself!

3 tbsp olive oil
160g (5oz) cooked, puréed pumpkin
(to make purée, roast pumpkin in the oven then put the flesh in a blender)
175g (6oz) honey
3 heaped tbsp brown sugar
2 eggs, beaten
115g (4oz) wholemeal flour
58g (2oz) plain flour
58g (2oz) chopped Kentish cobnuts
58g (2oz) sultanas
? tsp baking powder
? tsp each of cinnamon, nutmeg and allspice
A pinch of salt

METHOD

Grease and line a medium-sized loaf tin and pre-heat oven to 180°C (350°F, gas 4). Place the pumpkin purée, olive oil, brown sugar, honey and eggs in a large bowl and blend together. Add the flours, baking powder, spices and salt and blend well. Mix in the sultanas and pour the mixture into the loaf tin. Sprinkle the chopped cobnuts on top and place the loaf in the oven for approximately 55 minutes.

Remove from the oven and leave to cool in the tin for 10 minutes, then turn the loaf out onto a wire rack. When completely cool, slice the teabread and enjoy, either as it comes or spread with a little butter.

Kentish Cobnut & Mushroom Soup

A delicious combination of woodland flavours, all in a bowl of hot, satisfying, chunky soup.

50g (2oz) butter
3 tbsp plain flour
1 litre (1¾ pints) milk
3 tsp olive oil
2 onions, chopped
180g (6oz) mushrooms, sliced
50g (2oz) roasted Kentish cobnuts, finely chopped
A clove of garlic, crushed or finely chopped
125ml (4fl oz) single cream
2 tsp fresh mixed herbs, finely chopped
A twist of freshly ground black pepper

METHOD

Heat the butter in a large saucepan. When melted, add the flour and stir together over the heat for about one minute. Remove the saucepan from the cooker and gradually stir in the milk. Once mixed together smoothly, return the pan to the heat and bring to the boil, stirring continuously. When the sauce has thickened, remove the pan from the heat.

In a separate large saucepan, cook the onions and garlic in the olive oil, for about two minutes. Add the sliced mushrooms and fresh herbs and cook for a further three minutes. Stir in the white sauce and simmer together for 10 minutes. When cooked, use a slatted spoon to remove two large spoonfuls of the sliced mushrooms and set these aside. Blend the remaining soup until smooth. Finally, add the cream, chopped cobnuts, reserved mushrooms and a twist of freshly ground black pepper. Stir the soup over a low heat and serve when thoroughly warmed through.

Wild fruity yoghurt!

Make your own, it's quick and easy, it's as simple as one, two three! ...and great tasting too
Joyce Parker-Sarioglu explains

If you've got ten minutes spare, then you have time to sip a cup of tea before starting on yoghurt-making using the latest machines – the process really is that quick and easy!

The average person is dangerously short of culture – so says literature on yoghurt and, while that is obviously eye catching, it's actually not that far from the truth!

Today's society and food preparation methods mean the balance of our stomach's good bacteria is upset, and eating fresh yoghurt can assist in getting that balance back in order. This in turn means you'll benefit from the food's legendary health properties.

Yoghurt, it is claimed, can assist in everything from speeding up digestion, to reducing cholesterol.

Great health reasons for yoghurt consumption

- lowers cholesterol
- assists in the digestion of foods
- assists in the synthesis of vitamins
- low in calories
- low in fat
- good source of protein and calcium

Basically yoghurt is milk that has been thickened by bacteria and it is these bacteria that assist in the digestion and synthesis of foods. Research has been extensive and even shows that yoghurt consumption can guard

> "The average person is dangerously short of culture"

the intestinal tract from carcinogens as well as helping to heal ulcers and various digestive disorders. If that seems a little far-fetched, consider the importance of protein, using just one example, in the rebuilding of damaged tissue. Sportsmen have long understood how protein repairs muscles after particularly hard training sessions, likewise yoghurt can play a role when it comes to repairing damage that everyday life can cause.

Experts will tell you: "Only yoghurt containing live and active cultures (lactic bacteria) have the full benefits for your health."

> "Only yoghurt containing live and active cultures have the full benefits for your health"

Home-made

It's just as easy to do-it-yourself if you have a thermos flask, microwave or airing cupboard.

1 Buy some natural yoghurt. Make sure it is 'live'
2 Using sterilized milk, mix in a third of a cup of your yoghurt
3 Pour into small plastic containers and incubate overnight in a thermos or warm place at around 110-115°F – an airing cupboard is ideal

Easiyo Yoghurt Maker

This makes a variety of styles of yoghurt that involve no more than boiling water and the pre-supplied packet.

1 Mix up the contents of your packet with cold water
2 Place in the storage container that has been filled with boiling water
3 Allow to stand for eight hours and then chill. The yoghurt is then ready

Mix contents thoroughly...

Half fill with cold drinking water

Pour over boiling water

Pop it in

EasiYo retails at £13.99, or £20.40 for a complete starter kit. For details of your nearest stockist phone 01332 853577

Who should eat yoghurt

- Those who are lactose intolerant, especially the very young and the elderly
- Those on antibiotics or other strong drugs
- Those needing to reduce their intake of fat or production of cholesterol
- Pregnant and lactating mothers with their need of extra nutrients
- Those living with stress, or people who have a busy lifestyle
- Those who wish to increase their intake of calcium or protein
- The elderly who have slower digestion and decreased ability to assimilate some foods
- Those with a poor diet or bad digestion
- Those who over-exert themselves physically

Here are a few ideas to consider

Fresh yoghurt has infinite uses: salad dressings, jacket potatoes, toppings for vegetables, dips, even pasta sauces, mixed with fruit as a desert or as a topping for breakfast cereals.

When making your wild fruity yoghurt, it is important to remember not to add any fruit until after you have made the yoghurt as this will inhibit the process. Yoghurt can be frozen, but will alter in consistency after thawing, so is best used only in cooked or made up dishes.

Wild fruity yoghurt

875g (31oz) mixed wild fruits (raspberries, strawberries, elderberries, blackberries, damsons and gages)
150g (5oz) caster sugar
75ml (2½ fl oz) water

Wash and de-stalk your fruit and put into a saucepan with the sugar and water. Heat gently until the juices begin to run. Stir until the sugar has dissolved and cook until all the fruit is just tender. Remove from the heat and add the strawberries and raspberries.

Once cooled mix a couple of spoonfuls of the fruit mixture into some fresh yoghurt, pour into glasses and serve. You can freeze the fruit mixture to use throughout the winter months.

Alternatively you can put some yoghurt into a bowl and spoon the fruit mixture on top.

Elderberries

Elderberries are very high in vitamin C, they also have a good amount of potassium, iron and calcium in them. They are usually available for a good couple of months before they are too withered and wrinkled to be picked. Fresh berries can also be frozen for use later in the year. The berries are famously made into a country wine and can also be eaten freshly picked. There are many other uses for this berry, as **Peter Litfoot** explains

Elderberry ice lollies (or smoothies)

So long as you have a good liquidizer this is a good quick recipe which requires no addition of sugar. It is also non-dairy. Blackberries can be found at the same time as elderberries; the two fruits go well together in a number of recipes. The kiwi fruit and banana are very good due to their vitamin content, the banana also helps to add flavour to the lollies.

To make 8 lollies (or more if they are small)

1 medium sized ripe banana
1 kiwi fruit
100g (3½oz) blackberries
100g (3½oz) raspberries
100g (3½oz) elderberries
250ml (½ pint) water
Handful of ice cubes

METHOD
Wash the fruit. Peel the kiwi fruit and remove the hard central core if necessary. Peel the banana. Pull the elderberries off the stalks and pop into liquidizer with the other fruits, the water and the ice.

Liquidize thoroughly, adding extra water if needed – sometimes the fruit and ice soaks up the water to the extent that the liquidizer does not work properly. Fill the lolly moulds with the mixture leave to set overnight and enjoy on a hot day! If you have any surplus it can be drunk as a smoothie, perhaps by being slightly diluted with water depending on how thick you like them.

Beware that young children will, while enjoying these healthy treats, often make quite a mess with them!

Elderberry and blackberry jam

It's not important about the exact quantities of either the elderberries or blackberries, so long as, between them, you get enough together for the recipe.

2ltr jug full of de-stalked elderberries and blackberries
1.5 kg (3lb) sugar
50ml (2fl oz) vinegar

METHOD
Wash all the elderberries to ensure there are no creepy crawlies being added by accident. Put all the berries into a large pan and crush with a potato masher or other similar utensil. Bring the crushed berries to the boil on a high heat, add the sugar and vinegar and stir well. Any scum that rises to the surface while boiling should be skimmed off with a large spoon or ladle. Pour the mixture into boiled/sterilized jars and leave to cool.

Pear and elderberry chutney

This is a recipe you can make a little earlier than some of the others shown here as under-ripe berries are ideal here whereas you really need good fully ripe berries for most other recipes.

600g (1lb 6oz) destalked elderberries
2 pears cored and diced
2 medium onions, diced
125g (4oz) raisins
125g (4oz) sugar
500ml (18 fl oz) vinegar
2 tsp salt
A pinch of pepper
A pinch of mixed spice

METHOD
Aside from the sugar and half of the vinegar, put all of the other ingredients into a pan, and simmer on a low heat for around 30 minutes by which time the mixture should have thickened. Add the remaining vinegar, stir well and continue to simmer for a further 20 minutes, then add the sugar and simmer for a further 10 minutes. Mix well with a wooden spoon, if no liquid is visible in the pan it is ready to be put into sterile jars, otherwise simmer gently for a little longer. The chutney is best left to mature in the jars for at least three months before eating, making it an excellent Christmas present!

Elderberry and wild hedgerow pie

For the shortcrust pastry
200g (7oz) flour
50g (2oz) caster sugar
125g (4oz) butter
60ml (2 fl oz) cold water
Yolk of one egg

For the filling
200g (7oz) elderberries
200g (7oz) blackberries
200g (7oz) damsons or wild gauges
125g (¼lb) sugar
Grated rind of one lemon

To make the pastry
Rub the butter into the flour until it is the consistency of breadcrumbs. Mix in the sugar, add egg yolk and water. Mix to a stiff dough. Wrap in cling film and leave in the fridge for 30 minutes before rolling out to make the pie crust.

To make the pie
Grease a pie dish with a little butter and line with the pastry. De-stone the damsons or wild gauges and mix with the berries, half of the sugar and the rind of the lemon. Fill the pie with the fruit, sprinkle the remaining sugar on top and bake in a preheated oven at 210ºC (400ºF, gas 6) to properly cook the pastry, then reduce the heat to 190ºC (375ºF, gas 5) and cook for a further 15 minutes.

Elderberry jelly

1.5 kg (3lb) de-stalked elderberries
1.2 kg (2.5lb) sugar
Half a teaspoon of butter
50ml (2 fl oz) lemon juice
5 gelatine leaves, pre-soaked until soft

METHOD
Crush the fruit in a pan and cook on a medium heat until the juice comes out of the fruit. Reduce to a low heat, add the sugar and stir until it dissolves. Cover and simmer for a further 20 minutes, stirring occasionally and removing any scum that rises to the top. Leave to cool and strain off the fruit using a jelly bag or muslin cloth. Re-heat the syrupy liquid to a strong boil and add the gelatine leaves and stir them into the syrup until they have completely dissolved. Continue stirring for another minute or so still at full boil. Sterilize jars as for jam making in boiling water before pouring in the hot jelly, seal and leave to cool.

Elderberry cordial

2 ltr destalked elderberries
1kg (2lb) Sugar
1 tsp cloves

METHOD
Put the elderberries in a large pan, add water so that the fruit is just covered and stew for 15 minutes on a medium heat. Strain off the fruit and add the sugar and cloves and boil for a further 15 minutes. Allow to cool and pour in to sterile bottles and seal. If using plastic bottles the cordial can be frozen for use later in the year.

Autumn

Apples

Damsons

Sloe

Seeds

Fungi

Sweet chestnuts

Pheasants

Rabbit

Pigeon

Venison

Dandilion

Burdock

Seasonal Fruit
Apples

"But I, when I undress me
each night, upon my knees,
will ask the Lord to bless me,
with apple pie and cheese'.

Eugene Field

The apple occupies a firm position as one of the most favoured fruits – and one that can make a considerable contribution to a variety of dishes. Apples are commonly found on wasteground and the truely wild crab apple is widely found in hedgerows. Not only giving rise to puddings in a number of forms, they also combine well with various meats. In other incarnations, such as cider and the unique and delicious Calvados, they provide the absolute essence of a great meal.

Any old apples?

Well, as almost always, yes and no. On the 'yes' side, you can certainly make use of windfalls, retrieved battered and bruised from the ground, and similarly, those fruit half-devoured by insects and birds while still on the tree. By the time you've cut away any unwholesome parts, there's often a good few slices of fruit to be taken, which are perfectly good on the 'waste not, want not' basis. They won't be noticed at all within a finished dish.

Dessert apples or cookers – does it matter?

Up to a point it does, because cookers are sort of designed for the job. They are generally bigger and firmer, more sour and usually need to have some form of sweetening added to bring their flavour out and do the dish justice. More generations of small, ink-stained scrumpers have sat in trees, unhappily biting into something

attractively bright green that actually tastes like battery acid, pretending to each other that they like it, than you would believe.

However, it's quite possible to use dessert apples for a number of puddings, especially if you don't have cookers to hand. Many dessert apples have a slightly softer texture, and cooking times can be reduced accordingly, although other constituent parts of a dish such as pastry will need to be taken into account. You will also need less sweetening.

When you're using uncooked apples, it's very much a matter of personal taste. You definitely wouldn't want to find chunks of cooking apple in a fruit salad but, on the other hand, neither do you really want particularly soft–textured ones, either. Try out different varieties whenever possible and see what goes best with what. Keep a note of anything you particularly like and do try local produce – this may well have the advantage of being regularly available, while offerings from foreign climes can disappear whenever their price becomes disadvantageous to the supermarkets. Farm shops and markets also often sell fruit which has an irregular shape or scarring, which in no way affects the flavour, but can be reflected in the price, proving to be very good value for money.

It's sensible, too, to be selective about the apples you serve with cheese, with which the fruit goes fantastically well, simply because here the apple is eaten raw and there's no benefit of hidden sweetening or flavouring. Those with a slightly sharp tang are probably best with the creamier and more delicate cheeses, while milder

tasting apples offer a suitable accompaniment to something like a Cheddar with attitude.

Peel and quarter apples for people to eat and use unpeeled segments for decoration.

A worldwide product

We looked to see what apples were on offer in the shops. A check on the shelves of the local supermarket revealed quite a fair selection from Chile, China, South Africa and the United States. We only found one dessert apple from England, but there were unnamed English cooking apples and sealed packets of Bramleys.

Bramleys are notably excellent cookers of course and, if you can get them or grow them yourself, you will invariably obtain good results in the kitchen. However, there are lots of alternatives – literally hundreds of different varieties of apples are grown, though one suspects that the choice in the supermarkets is limited by price criteria more than anything else.

Modern storage

Freezing is by far the most effective means of storing apples. They need to be kept in a sugar and water syrup – this should contain ascorbic acid (lemon juice is the most easily procured source of this, but you can get powder or crystals from chemists) to keep the fruit from discolouring. Peel, core and chop or slice before freezing – there's no point in wasting space on bits you don't want anyway – and pack into bags or plastic containers. Generally speaking, apples will keep satisfactorily frozen for about a year.

Apple sauce

Apple sauce is traditionally served with both pork and goose. While you can get away with simply stewing the apples and adding a little sugar to taste, it's better by far to take the time and trouble to prepare this properly.

To make sufficient for four people, chop half a medium onion very finely and soften this in either butter or lard in a heavy pan for five minutes. Peel, core and slice a couple of apples and add them to the onion in the pan, together with a dessertspoonful of sugar and a couple of tablespoonsful of dry cider. Stir things up, cover the pan and let the apples cook down until they break up into fluffy bits, then take the pan off the heat.

You can use water instead of cider and a couple of cloves – or half a teaspoon of ground cloves – can be added with the apples before cooking if you like the extra flavour.

Take the whole cloves out after cooking if you've used them and beat the sauce until it becomes completely smooth. Grate a little nutmeg (again, if you like the taste) over the sauce and serve.

Baked apple pudding

Can you imagine a finer way to warm yourself up?

1.5kg (3lb) of apples
175g (6oz) of sugar
90g (3oz) of butter
3 eggs
A pint of fresh breadcrumbs and a few cloves.

Peel, core and slice the apples as you would for a sauce and boil them gently with the cloves until they are soft. Remove the cloves, melt the butter and whisk the eggs, then add both to the apples and beat together for a minute or two.

Butter a pie dish and put in a layer of breadcrumbs, followed by a layer of the apple mixture, alternating these until the dish is filled, but making sure you finish with a layer of breadcrumbs on the top.

Flake a few small pieces of butter over the pudding and bake in the oven at 180°C (350°F, Gas 4) for about half-an-hour, or until the top is golden and crunchy.

If you like, a few drops of lemon juice or some thin, small pieces of lemon peel can be added to the apples. You're not likely to get many complaints if you serve the pudding with ice cream or custard, either.

The versatility of apples

Apple pancakes

These are well worth a go, but then we would say that! They are very quick and easy to prepare and something children enjoy eating. If you like you can sprinkle some extra sugar over them and serve them hot with ice- cream.

Makes two big fat pancakes

3 medium sized dessert apples
4 tbsp plain flour
1 tbsp cooking oil
½ tbsp sugar
3 eggs
200ml (7 fl oz) milk
½ tsp cinnamon

METHOD

Mix all the ingredients except the apples into a smooth batter. Core, peel and chop the apples into small chunks. Heat the oil on a medium heat in a large pan. Mix the apples with the batter and pour into pan. Cook for five minutes, then taking care to turn the pancake, turn the heat down to low and cook for 8-10 minutes. Tip: turn the pancake by placing a plate on top of the pan and flipping it on to the plate, you can then slide it back into the pan to cook the other side.

Heaven and Earth

Peel and chop 1kg (2lb) of potatoes and 500g (18oz) of cooking apples. Boil the potatoes until tender. Meanwhile, heat around 150g (5oz) of diced streaky bacon with a small, chopped onion in a heavy pan. When the bacon is crisp, remove it and add the potato and apple to the pan, cooking until the apple is softened and the potatoes are hot and going brown.

Season with salt and pepper, sprinkle the bacon over all and serve – sausages or black pudding are recommended as accompaniments.

Apple dumplings

A different take on individual apple pie. Simply peel and core a suitable number of apples.

Fill the apples with sugar – possibly dusting in a little ground cinnamon as well – and wrap them in squares cut from a crust of suet pastry.

(Two thirds plain flour to one third suet, with a little water to bind.)

Mould the dumplings with your hands so they become round, put on a tray and bake for around 30 minutes at 180°C (350°F, Gas 4), or a little longer if you're using really large apples. Dust them all over with sugar immediately before serving with single cream.

Apple tart

This tart is so simple to make, and yet it ends up looking so impressive, and tasting so impressive! Why not make two, and freeze one for later in the season.

Serves 4

500g (18oz) cooking apples
300g (10oz) short crust pastry (see below)
200g (7oz) Demerara (or other brown) sugar
½ tsp cinnamon
50g (2oz) butter

Short crust pastry recipe
You can buy short crust pastry ready made, but it's not difficult to make it yourself.

200g (7oz) flour
50g (2oz) caster sugar
125g (4½oz) butter
1tsp ground cinnamon
4x15ml (½ fl oz) cold water
Yolk of one egg

METHOD FOR PASTRY
Rub the butter into the flour and cinnamon until it is the consistency of fine breadcrumbs. Mix in the sugar, add egg yolk and water. Mix to a stiff dough. Do not over-handle or the pastry will be tough. Wrap in clingfilm and leave to rest in the fridge for half an hour or so before using it.

METHOD FOR TART
Grease a tart dish with butter and line with pastry. Core, peel and slice the apples thickly. Overlap the sliced apple in the dish, dust with cinnamon and completely cover with the sugar. Put the butter on the top of the tart in small dabs. Bake in a pre heated oven at 210°C (400°F, Gas 6) to properly cook the pastry, then reduce heat to 190°C (375°F, Gas 5) and cook for a further 15 minutes.

Baked apples

The cinnamon works so well with this easy pudding. Just make sure you use apples that look good since you will not be peeling them.

4 large apples
4 tbsp water
Demerara (or other brown) sugar
Butter
Cinnamon

METHOD
Remove the cores of the apples with a corer or a sharp knife, leaving the rest of the apple intact. Rub a pinch of cinnamon around the inside of the apples and stand them in an oven dish and pour 150ml (¼ pint) of water around them. Fill the centres with the sugar, place a dab of butter on the tops, cover them with silver foil and pop into a preheated oven at 200°C (400°F, Gas 6) for 45 minutes. Remove from oven to eat either hot or cold. Pour the sauce from the dish over the apple before serving and serve with ice cream or cream

Baked apples with berries

For a special, tasty and colourful version of baked apple, try adding your favourite berries.

Ingredients as for baked apple above except add seasonal berries.

METHOD
As above except remove the apples from the oven after 30 minutes, put berries into the cavities and top with another teaspoon of sugar

Upside-down apple pie (Tarte tartin)

We all love apple pie don't we? And this is certainly the season to be making them. In France, every little cafe, and every grand restaurant will offer Tarte Tartin. I make this dish all the year round, a classic recipe and like most classics, simple honest food. The only problem is stopping my husband from eating the whole pie in one go. Like all classics, cooks will make their own adjustments to the recipe, this is my version. You will need a tartin tin, usually a round metal dish with two handles, rather like a paella dish about 10cms -15cms in diameter. You could use a small frying pan with an ovenproof handle.

Serves 4 – 6 (or one husband)

1 packet of ready-made puff pastry
1 kilo (2lb) Granny Smith apples, or similar, peeled, cored, halved, quartered and sliced, and placed into lemon water.
Zest of one lemon.
110g (3½oz) butter
110g (3½oz) brown sugar

METHOD

Melt the butter and sugar in your pan on the hob. Add the apple slices, remember that this will be the top of the pie, so arrange carefully, you may want to arrange the slices in circles for a more fancy finished dish. Add the lemon zest. Place the dish on a high heat back on the hob. Cook for 5-7 minutes, the smell will change to a lovely caramelly apple perfume, and the apples will darken. This is essential. Watch this last step carefully. When this happens, remove from the heat and allow to cool for a few minutes. Roll out the pastry, and cover the dish, tucking any excess under like a blanket.

Put in the oven at 200°C (400°F, gas 6) for about 30 minutes. The pastry will rise and rise. Remove from the oven, cool for a few minutes. Then, carefully cover the cooking dish with your selected serving dish, and turn over so that your pie emerges right way up, apples on top. Serve with sweetened creme fraiche. The perfect pudding with any of the roasts.

Juicing

"It is quite incredible seeing all the liquid flooding out, you must make sure that the container collecting the juice is big enough!"

The fruits of your labour!

If you find you have an overwhelming supply of apples and don't want to see them wasted, then you could consider juicing them. You simply cannot beat home-made apple juice, freshly pressed and chilled. And when juicing you can use all the apples that are not fit to be stored, windfalls and apples that 'others' have already had a go at. If you want to juice but don't have a ready supply at hand, many farm shops, at this time of year, will sell very cheap boxes of 'less than perfect' apples, often known as 'horse apples'. These are however, perfect for juicing.

Getting started

There are two essential pieces of kit you need to buy or borrow. The first is a fruit crusher and the second is a fruit press. Don't be tempted into thinking that all you need is a press – pressing apples without first passing them through the crusher will yield you very little juice at all. We used a press and crusher from Vigo Ltd to crush and press our apples and found that we were able to get 3 litres of apple juice from every 10kg of apples.

The crusher

This unit literally chews up and, to a certain extent mashes, the apples. Simply halve or quarter the apples and load them into the hopper. This is something that children very much enjoy getting involved in. That's all okay and good fun, but you must make sure they are old enough to understand that they don't put their fingers in the hopper; the moving parts that mash up the apples are much stronger than adults, let alone childrens', fingers.

We found it best to crush our apples into a large (25 litre) bucket, and then once crushed deal with the pressing.

One box of apples thoroughly crushed

The fruit press

When loading the fruit press, ensure that before you start you have a container in place to catch the juice, as it may well start to flow even before you begin pressing. Fill the press right to the top with the crushed fruit, then compact it down by hand and top up until you can no longer get any more fruit in. Next put the two halves of the round wooden lid on top of the fruit and push down again. The press we used was supplied with a further three chocks of wood (including a larger one which screws onto the top of the press), we found it useful to use yet more chocks here, so that we were only just able to screw the turning handle on to the press. Without these extra chocks of wood we were only able to press the fruit so far before the handle reached the top of the press.

It is quite incredible to see all the liquid flooding out, you must make sure that the container collecting the juice is big enough!

Another tip, we would pass on here, is to press the fruit as much as you can, and when you think you can turn the handle no more, have a break for a few minutes. Then have another really determined go at it, you may find, like we did, that there was another 15% or more juice to be had out of the pulp.

Once all your pulp has been pressed, you can then filter the juice through a sieve or muslin to extract any bits and pieces and then decant the juice into storage bottles. You can use plastic or glass, we found plastic milk cartons (plastic, not the cardboard type) useful here in order to freeze the juice. These cartons are good and flexible enough to allow for a little expansion in the freezer. The equipment we used was relatively easy to clean as it all comes apart for easy access. The pulp, at the end of the day can then be composted. Alternatively, if you are fortunate to have any chickens, pigs or horses, a bucket full of pulp would certainly make them a tasty treat.

Making cider

You can make cider simply by adding yeast to your pressed apple juice, since there is natural sugar in the apples. To do this warm the apple juice to around 20-22°C. Add yeast and leave it in a warm place in a sterile bucket with a damp cloth over the top. Expect to see rather a lot of frothing in the first few days, after which you should be able to transfer into a demijohn and fit an air lock for the remainder of the fermentation. After around two weeks the cider should be ready to decant, chill and drink. For a stronger cider you could add at the start a kilo of sugar for every 4 litres of juice, in which case the fermentation could take three weeks or more. ●

A helping hand is always welcome!

We found extra chocks of wood useful in order to press more juice out

That was thirsty work!

Crab Apples

They may be too sour to eat from the trees, but crab apples still have a long tradition of being put to good use in the kitchen. Here are some ideas for you to consider.

Crab apples are frequently found in mature oak woodlands or throughout the country in hedges. They are not like ordinary apples, the fruit being much smaller and very bitter. They flower in the early spring, like every other apple species, and fruits later in the summer.

The yield of the plant per bush is very similar to that of the other apples, but because they are small there is more seed in comparison to the amount of flesh.

It is said that the fruit gets it's 'crab' name because they generally appear like crabs dotted around on the ground, perhaps thier sharp bitterness also had some influence here. There are those who like to eat the fruit in its raw state, but you are likely to get a tummy ache unless you happen to be one of those few with a cast iron stomach.

Using the fruit

Crab apples are good to add to other apples in all sorts of dishes. They add sharpness and a depth of flavour, a little like a seasoning. Also, crab apple wine is rich in acidity and vitamin C. You will need to add a lot of sugar to make this wine, but the fruit will make the yeast work extremely well, and crab apple wine is always very potent.

Of course the basic reason for collecting crab apples is to make jelly. This condiment goes well with savour as well as sweet dishes. In particular, crab apple jelly with scones and cream on a summer's afternoon, is an gastronomical delight not to be turned down.

Pickled Crab Apples

4 litres (7 pints) crab apples
3 sticks cinnamon
3 tsp whole cloves
600ml (1 pint) vinegar
800g (1¾lbs) sugar

METHOD

Select apples that are in the best condition and pick them with the stalks attached, wash them and remove the blossom ends, but leave the stalks.

Put the spices into a muslin bag and tie together.

Heat up the vinegar to boiling point, add the sugar and stir to dissolve, add the spices and boil for a further five minutes. Turn the heat down to a gentle simmer and add the apples. Simmer very gently to avoid the skin splitting open and cook until the apples soften, about ten minutes. Remove the apples from the pan leaving the vinegar syrup behind, pack the apples into sterilized jars, then pour in the syrup to around 1cm below the lid. Seal the jars.

Crab apple jelly

The cinnamon works so well with this easy pudding. Just make sure you use apples that look good since you will not be peeling them.

1 ltr (2 pints) crab apples, unpeeled
Sugar according to measurement
1 tsp groun cinnamon

METHOD

Clean the apples, removing any stalks and flowers. Chop the fruit but do not peel and place in a heavy bottomed pan. Just cover with water and boil until the fruit is very soft. Filter the liquid into a bowl using a jelly bag. Do not be tempted to squeeze the bag! This should take a good few hours. Measure the volume of the liquid and for each 250 ml of juice add 250 g of sugar and bring to the boil. Continue to heat until the whole mixture starts to reduce. Carefully ladle the jelly into sterilised jars and put a jam disc in place to seal. When cooled, close with a metal lid.

Damsons and greengages

Wendy Riddell discovers the wonder of these lovely fruits

Damsons are a blue-black oval fruit which look very much like plums, they have a lovely soft blue bloom and. They were first found growing in Damascus by the Crusaders around 2000 years ago, they are responsible for bringing them to Europe.

The greenish-yellow flesh can be eaten raw but only when fully ripe, they do tend to have more stone than fruit so are best eaten cooked in a pie or crumble or preserved, they do make excellent homemade wine.

The greengage is a small, round, green plum with a golden, sweet, scented flesh. It is thought that wild greengages were first introduced to Britain by the Romans, but it was Sir Thomas Gage who first cultivated the fruit in Britain. He lived in Suffolk where the growing conditions are perfect for this mouth-watering fruit. They do make excellent jam or purées for pies and puddings.

Pork chop with plums or greengages

500g (1lb) plums or greengages, stoned
60g (2oz) sugar
Pinch of ground allspice
225ml (8fl oz) red wine
4 pork chops
Salt and pepper

METHOD
Put the plums or greengages into a saucepan with the sugar, allspice and wine and bring to the boil. Simmer for 10 to 15 minutes or until fruit is tender. Meanwhile rub the chops with salt and pepper and grill for 4 minutes on each side or until slightly browned. Transfer the chops to an ovenproof serving dish. Put the fruit mixture through a strainer or sieve and pour over the chops. Cover with a tight fitting lid and put into a pre-heated moderate oven 180°C (350°F, gas 4). Cook for 45 minutes to 1 hour or until the chops are tender.

Very easy one crust pie

For the shortcrust pastry
175g (6oz) plain flour
40g (1¼oz) lard, at room temperature
40g (1¼oz) butter or margarine, at room temperature
Cold water

For the filling
750g (1½lb) prepared fruit, any kind rhubarb, gooseberries, raspberries, plums or damsons
90g (3oz) caster sugar
2tbsp semolina
1 small egg yolk, lightly beaten

For the glaze
1 small egg white, lightly whisked
6 sugar cubes, crushed

METHOD

Lightly grease a solid baking sheet. Make up the pastry by sifting all the flour into a large bowl then rubbing the fats in lightly with your fingertips, lifting everything up and letting it fall back into the bowl to give it a good airing. When the mixture reaches the crumb stage sprinkle in enough cold water to bring it together to a smooth dough, which leaves the bowl clean with no crumbs left. Give it a little light knead to bring it fully together, then place the pastry in a polythene bag in the fridge for 30 minutes. Pre-heat the oven to 200°C (400°F, gas 6), then roll the pastry out on to a flat surface to around approx 35cm (14 inches) as you roll give it quarter turns so that it ends up as round as you can. Don't worry though about ragged edges, they're fine. Now carefully roll the pastry round the rolling pin and transfer it to the centre of the baking sheet. To prevent the pastry getting soggy from excess juice paint the inside base with egg yolk, you'll need to cover approx a 25cm (10inch) circle in the centre. Then sprinkle the semolina lightly over, the semolina is there to absorb the juices and the egg yolk provides a waterproof coating. Now simply pile up the prepared fruit in the centre of the pastry sprinkling it with sugar as you go. Then all you do is turn in the edges of the pastry, if any breaks appear, just patch it back on again, it's all meant to be ragged and interesting. Brush the pastry surface all round with egg white then crush the sugar cubes with a rolling pin and sprinkle over the pastry, this gives a less uniform look than with granulated sugar. Pop the pie on the highest shelf of the oven and bake for approx 35 minutes or until the crust is golden brown. Remove from the oven and serve warm with chilled crème fraiche or ice cream.

Damson jam

Delicious with scones and cream!

500g (1lb) sugar to 500g (1lb) damsons and 1 litre (1¾pint) water

METHOD

Pick over the damsons and remove any stalks. Wash them and drain thoroughly. Put them into a pan with a little water and cook over a low heat until the juice runs out of the fruit. When there is enough juice to prevent the fruit from sticking bring gently to boiling point. Now add in the slightly warmed sugar, stir well and boil rather quickly until a little jam tested on a cold plate sets well. While the jam is boiling pick out as many stones as you can. They will rise to the top as the syrup bubbles. Use a perforated spoon to avoid waste. Bottle into warmed sterilised jars.

Sloe or damson gin

This can be made with damsons, slightly earlier in the year or even raspberries if you use vodka instead of gin. Traditionally this should be kept for at least six months before drinking (but you're unlikely to get any complaints if it's opened early, after your Christmas meal!)

75cl bottle
500g (1lb) sloes or damsons
300g (10oz) sugar

Prick the fruit several times with a needle and drop into an empty bottle. If the fruit are too big to fit into the neck without being crushed, use a wide-necked preserving jar and then decant into small presentation bottles when ready. Add the sugar and top up with spirit. Tip the bottle up several times to start the sugar dissolving. Leave somewhere cool and dark for six months, turning occasionally. When ready, strain though a scalded muslin and decant into sterilised bottles.

Damson, port and rosemary jelly

If you have any plums in your freezer or manage to get the last of the damsons from the hedgerows this is a lovely jelly to accompany meat.

1kg (2lb) damsons
Sprig rosemary
Sugar
Port (I use tawny)

METHOD
Put the fruit into a pan and simmer with a little water until soft and pulpy. Strain overnight through a jelly bag. Pour juice into a measuring jug and top-up to nearest ½ litre with port. Return to a heavy-based pan and add as much sugar as you had liquid, so for example for one litre of juice, add one kilo of sugar. Add rosemary and bring to the boil, stirring constantly. Boil for one minute. Skim any scum from the top, remove the rosemary if you want, and then pour into warm sterilised jars.

Saving seeds

There are many reasons for collecting seeds from edible wild plants, not the least for growing them in your garden so you have a supply of excellent wild food on your doorstep

Collecting for planting out

If you are keeping seeds for planting out, you have to be sure the seed will last the winter out by keeping it in the right conditions. In the wild, seeds fall to the ground, or pass through an animal, and then germination is almost a matter of chance. Out of a hundred seeds only around ten to fifteen ever germinate. However, in the garden we are used to a much higher success rate, but to be able to achieve this we need to give the seed a little help. Damp is the enemy of seeds.

First of all, collect the seeds on a dry day, preferably the day after another dry day. Keep the seeds away from your hands, which will warm them. Wrap them in kitchen roll and then place this into a sealable envelope. Write the name of the seeds and the date they were collected on the front.

Then collect your envelopes into a sealable container and if you have the chance, put in one of those sachets of silica gel, which will take out all the moisture. Then seal up the container and place it in the freezer.

Seeds generally only germinate when ripe, so don't plant them straight away. Only collect healthy seeds, discard the rest.

Collecting seeds for food

You have to be careful when you collect seeds for consumption. Many of them contain tannins and cyanide, which may at best give you a tummy upset. Be careful particularly with red coloured woods seeds. The following, however, are perfectly edible.

Cobnut

These are a special kind of hazelnut, mostly grown in Kent. It is such an easy job to collect and eat fresh. You can simply place them into moist ground and they will germinate readily too.

There is no need to dry cobnuts, unlike walnuts, and they will keep fresh for ages, and you can keep the brown shell in place until you need to use the nut.

Sweet chestnut

These look a little like a conker, but the seeds are smaller. You can recognise the tree by the bark, which is deeply grooved in a spiral. They were brought by the Romans to the UK and harvested with a hooked stick. The one piece of invaluable equipment in the countryside is the stick, and you shouldn't enter a field without one, if only to thwart the charging of the odd ram.

The Romans made these nuts into flour, but we tend to roast them and eat straight away, or add to stuffing or roasts. Split the skin before you roast them, otherwise they will go off like a firecracker!

Sunflower

This is not a wild plant, but it should be grown by everyone just for the seeds. I use the whole head to feed to my hens, which peck away at the seeds directly from the large disc. However, there are few seeds more useful to mankind, in salads and roasts and dishes of all kinds.

I fill an old sweet container with the seeds for my own use and those left at the bottom get planted again for next year, in a plastic coffee cup of moist compost.

Acorns

The history of the oak is inextricably linked to the pig. Its spread came about by pigs eating acorns and squashing them into the ground. The foot of the pig's trotter is ideal for picking up acorns and as the pigs move around the countryside they planted acorns all over.

Acorns are collected from their cups and have to be processed before eating. They are so full of tannin that they would give you stomach cramps if you were to eat them raw. They need to be crushed and soaked in many changes of water for around 24 hours. They can then be ground and used with flour to make buns or used to make patties.

Nasturtium

These are not nuts exactly, but the fruits of nasturtium can be collected and pickled in vinegar. They make a fantastic condiment and an excellent replacement for capers. They are slightly peppery and give you wind – so watch out!

Poppy

The elaborate shakers on the garden poppy seem to me to be the best container for keeping the seeds. I collect the heads and tape up the holes in the fruit until I need to use the seeds; normally on the top side of bread buns. The seeds can be collected into envelopes for sowing in the spring.

Rowan

The Mountain Ash is a large tree that looks a little like a birch, except that the bark is different. The fruits are bright red and are quite edible. You will find them with seeds in, but the fruits can be turned into jellies – great at Christmas. You need to separate the seeds from the flesh by pushing it through a sieve.

Main pic: Burdock seeds are very easy to collect and grow. Spinkle the seeds into a corner of the garden. The plant does not flower in its first year, but will do in the second. See page 128 for uses of Burdocks.

Nuts!

Cobnuts are very easy to grow, collect from August onwards and simply pop the nuts into pots and protect from squirrels and rabbits.

Sweet chestnuts should be collected in October and not allowed to dry out before planting in pots.

Walnuts can be picked from the trees in August and September. Later in the year you may find them like this around the base of the tree. Plant in pots and water regularly from Spring.

Foraging for fungus

Want to know what edible fungi are out there in the countryside just waiting to be harvested? If so, you should consider signing up for an expert-led tour. We did just that and went out with the fungus expert **John Wright** from River Cottage Headquarters in Dorset

John Wright picking up a large parasol

Events run at River Cottage really are special, you get treated so well, having the RCHQ chefs prepare a superb feast from your day's harvest. To ensure getting on to these events you should book up good and early (note that while Hugh Fearnley-Whittingstall takes an active role in some of the events, he does not normally come on these walks). If making it to Dorset is too far for you to travel, check out the alternatives, there are plenty of other regional events around to choose from.

Our day started at 9.30am with a full English breakfast at RCHQ. Somehow the term 'full English breakfast' doesn't seem to do justice to the hearty meal that set us up for a day's foraging on a blustery wet autumn day. Shortly after 10am we were whisked away by coach to begin our hunt.

On arrival bottles of water were handed out – essential to keep us hydrated for the duration of our three hour fungus collecting tour. Collection baskets and a healthy stash of homemade flapjacks were all part of our kit list for the day.

We soon got to our hunting ground, a sloping meadow which had not been ploughed for at least 15 to 20 years. The first find was a Crimson Wax Cap, which, like the name perhaps suggests, had a slimy or waxy feel to it. Our expert John told us that these can be eaten both cooked and raw. Almost immediately after this find, as the hunters spread out, we were discovering more and more varieties – literally all over the place. While this meadow was farmed, it was used as grazing land, and the lack of ploughing had allowed all these different species of fungus to become firmly established.

Snowy Wax Caps, and Yellow Wax Cap were next to be seen, closely followed by Meadow Wax Cap, at which John proclaimed – "now that's what I want you to find – this is the best of all the wax caps." The Meadow Wax Cap is orange coloured and makes particularly good eating. John's favourite fungus of all is the chanterelle, sadly this was one of the few popular species that we did not find on this day.

"...now that's what I want you to find – this is the best of all the wax caps."

Meadow Wax Cap

We found over 20 different species of fungi in this small meadow, most of which were not only edible, but very tasty too

Shaggy Parasols (the names just get more and more interesting!) were collected but we were told that some people are allergic to this

" ... they had the most amazing aniseed smell to them..."

variety, whereas there tends to be no problem associated with the Ordinary Parasol. As a rule, it is recommended that as well as being certain about exactly what fungus it is you have, you should try new species a little at a time. A reference book is always useful, our expert John has an extensive collection of books which he often refers to. Despite having led these trips for

years, when asked if he ever finds anything he's not seen before his reply was "Yes, every time!"

We found plenty of Horse Mushrooms and they had the most amazing aniseed smell to them, these tend to be quite common, and like the similar Field Mushroom are often found by walkers along footpaths through fields. Another very common species we found was the Fairy Ringed Champignon. These fairy fungus things are really common on garden lawns and can be quite prolific. Lots of people hate them as they can make a lawn look messy, however, I for one was certainly pleased to discover that they are absolutely delicious to eat. Be aware though, you must first make a positive identification here, there is a deadly fungus called *Clitocyke dealbata* that can be mistaken for Fairy Ring Champignons. Fairy Ring Champignons are easily identified by their tough, fibrous stem and their broadly spaced gills.

Heading off on the start of our mushroom hunt

Making our way into the ancient wood

Puff Balls

We were also told that all puff balls are perfectly edible as long as they are pure white inside. Simply take off the skin, slice up and fry the puff palls in butter for a few minutes, then add the egg to make an omelette – delicious. If you open one up and it is yellow or brown on the inside it is past its best and should not be used.

The ancient woods

After some time on the open meadow we headed into an ancient woodland to see what other varieties we could find. On our way we picked up a stash of watercress which is great for making soup (please note that it is recommended that wild watercress is cooked as there is a risk of liver fluke if eaten fresh).

It was in the woods that John explained a little more about fungi. The bits we were harvesting were just the fruits, the reproductive organs, of the fungus. The main part, which lies underground, consists of a massive network of fibres called a mycellium. These mycelia can grow to an enourmous size covering many square kilometers in some cases, making them by far the largest organisms on earth (beat that, Blue Whale!). Magic Mushrooms, by the way, are a class A drug. We didn't find any, had we done, interestingly, taking them would only have been illegal if we knew them to be Magic Mushrooms. Ignorance, in this instance, does seem to give you protection from the law.

It's all in the name

The Death Cap mushroom (they name some of these things really well) is the most dangerous of all fungi as it looks as though it could be edible. It has a green cap, which is quite common, but also a large bag at its base. This is one of the reasons why, when harvesting fungi, you should lift the whole thing including the base.

In the woods we found 'forests of Honey Fungus'. Apparently these are sometimes responsible for killing fruit trees, when asked what you could do about it (to save your fruit trees) the answer was "nothing, move house!". We also found a number of Bracket Fungi growing on the stumps of trees. Unlike Oyster mushrooms that grow in similar conditions, these are not edible. A simple way to tell the difference is to look at the underside. Oyster mushrooms have gills, Bracket Fungus doesn't.

Alcohol free zone

We also found a number of Ink-Caps, named because of the fact that as they age they ooze a black inky fluid from their caps! It was noted here that some Ink-Caps while perfectly edible, contain a dangerous toxin which is soluble when combined with alcohol. So, bear if mind if eating these ones you cannot drink alcohol!

The Velvet Shank

This is a really special fungus, as it contains a natural antifreeze. Not that you can use it in your car, but it is one of very few edible fungi that can still be harvested into the winter given that it is frost tolerant. We found several of these later in our hunt.

All good things come to an end, and before too long we were heading back to the coach with our bounty. Once back at RCHQ, John sorted out most of the edible stuff for the chefs to prepare them for the table (John also collected some non-edible specimens to help identify differences). Coffee and chocolate fudge brownies were given out and Ray Smith the famous RCHQ butcher, gave a talk and taste session on rabbit and venison. We all also tried a slice of wild mushroom frittata during this talk. Meanwhile an impressive display of collected specimens was being put together all labelled up with their Latin names! We were all impressed with the number of things we had managed to collect, all in one forage. After a talk and Q&A session on our collection we sat down to enjoy rabbit and wild mushroom stew served with sea beet gratin, followed by damson ice cream, shortbread and damsons preserved in gin. As I said earlier, they know how to treat guests down at River Cottage!

●

Selection of fungi collected on our day out

Popular wild fungi

Chanterelle
- Woodland
- Apricot smell
- Bright yellow

Field mushroom
- Meadow/grassland
- One ring around stem
- Familiar mushroom smell
- Have pink gills that turn brown then black

Cep
- Often found near oak and beech
- Large size, brown, have pores and tubes instead of gills
- Common

Wood Blewit
- Deciduous woodland
- Liliac purple colour
- Common

Horse mushroom
- Parks and meadows
- Creamy white
- Aniseed smell
- Has a large ring on the stem with "cogwheel" markings underneath when young

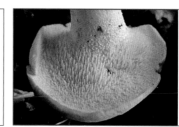

Hedgehog mushroom
- Broadleafed woodlands
- Irregular round shape
- Coloured from matt, cream to mustard yellow
- Has little spines underneath instead of gills

Parasol
- Common on meadow and grassland
- Pale with brown scales
- Has a ring on the stem which you can slide up and down
- Common

The Miller
- Found on meadows, grassland and open woods
- Smells strongly like flour, hence the name The Miller
- Pinkish gills run down the stem

Giant Puffball
- Common on pasture land sometimes found in woodland
- Large, occasionally irregular shape
- White, up to 80cm wide

Favourite mushrooms available in spring

St George's mushroom
- Fields, hedgerows, grassy woodlands
- Bright white, appear normally in late April
- Floury smell

Fairy Ring Champignon
- Lawns/grassland
- Pale to dark tan
- Commonly forms rings on lawns

Morels
- Woodland/old orchards
- Grey, yellow or black
- Honeycombed surface to caps

Further reading

These books are the best available to help in identification. The first is unaccountably out of print but try www.bookfinder.com, www.abebooks.com or www.amazon.co.uk for second hand copies. *Collins Field Guide to Mushrooms and Toadstools*, by R. Courtecuisse & B. Duhem – this is my favourite smaller guide. *The Mushrooms and Toadstools of Britain and North-Western Europe*, by Marcel Bon. A new edition is now over nine months overdue and should be available soon!

Mushrooms and other Fungi of Great Britain & Europe, by Roger Phillips (Again, a new edition should soon be available). *The Fungi of Switzerland* is in five volumes and at about £80 a shot is not a cheap option. Do not be put off by the "Switzerland" part as most of the fungi in the books can be found in the UK and Ireland. These books are precise and glorious, get them if you can. See also John's website www.wildmushrooms.info

Mushroom recipes

Wild mushroom and rabbit casserole

1 rabbit
1 onion, sliced
2 stalks of celery, chopped
2 medium carrots, chopped
50g (2oz) plain flour
50g (2oz) butter
100g (3½oz) wild mushrooms
250ml (8fl oz) chicken stock
Salt and pepper

METHOD

Joint the rabbit and toss in seasoned flour. Melt the butter in a frying pan and cook the rabbit til lightly browned. Set aside while you fry the onion until translucent but not brown. Add the celery and carrots and cook for a couple of minutes, then put them into an ovenproof dish with the onion, seasoning and rabbit. Add the stock, cover and cook at 180°C (360°F, gas 4) for an hour and a half, until the rabbit is tender. 20 minutes before the end, add the mushrooms, slicing any which are very large, and continue to cook for another half an hour or so, until the rabbit is tender.

Wild mushroom omelette

4 eggs, beaten
100g (3½oz) wild mushrooms
2 small, ripe tomatoes
Salt and freshly ground black pepper
Handful of herbs, chopped
Drizzle of oil
Knob of butter

METHOD

Gently heat the butter in a frying pan until melted, then add the mushrooms and fry gently until just tender. In the meantime, beat the eggs in a bowl and add the chopped herbs and salt and pepper. Slice the tomatoes. Add a drizzle of olive oil to the frying pan when the mushrooms are ready, and pour in the egg mixture. Add the tomato slices. Cook gently, without fiddling with it, until the top is just setting. At this point, you can either flip it over to brown the other side, or you can leave it as it is and just fold one half over the other. Sprinkle with chopped herbs to serve.

Breaded wild mushrooms

100g (3½oz) wild mushrooms, cut to uniform-ish sizes
100g (3½oz) plain flour, seasoned with salt and freshly ground black pepper
2 eggs, beaten
100g (3½oz) white breadcrumbs
500ml (18fl oz) oil

METHOD

Toss the mushrooms in the flour, coat them in egg, then roll in the breadcrumbs.

Heat the oil in a deep, heavy-bottomed pan until a piece of bread bubbles at the edge when dropped in. Fry the mushrooms until golden, then carefully remove with a slotted spoon and drain on kitchen paper.

Delicious served with garlic and herb sour cream dip.

Stuffed wild mushrooms

2 large flat mushrooms
1 garlic clove, peeled and crushed
50g (2oz) fresh breadcrumbs
Zest and juice of ½ lemon
2 sage leaves, finely chopped
25g (1oz) cheese, grated
Salt and freshly ground black pepper
Drizzle of olive oil

METHOD

Preheat the oven to 220° (425°F, gas 7). Put the mushrooms onto a baking tray. Mix the breadcrumbs, garlic, lemon, sage and seasoning together, and fill the mushrooms. Top with grated cheese and drizzle with a little olive oil. Roast in the oven for 8-10 minutes, or until the cheese is golden brown and bubbling.

Rabbit casserole with puffballs

1kg (2lb) rabbit, either jointed or diced
60g (2oz) flour
Handful of fresh thyme
Salt and pepper
225ml (8fl oz) white wine
2 garlic cloves, crushed
Butter
500g (1lb) puffballs, peeled and cut into thick slices

METHOD

Pre-heat the oven to 180°C (350°F, gas 4). Mix the flour, thyme, salt and pepper and dust the rabbit with the mixture. Lightly fry until golden, then transfer to an ovenproof dish.

Strip the thyme leaves from the stalk, into the frying pan, add the garlic and fry lightly for a couple of seconds. Pour in the wine and boil it to reduce and slightly thicken, for a couple of minutes. Pour it over the rabbit, cover and bake for 15-20 minutes.

While the rabbit is cooking, cut the puffballs into uniformly thick slices and gently fry them in butter until cooked – about five minutes, depending on the thickness of the slices. Add to the rabbit, and cook for a further 15 minutes.

Chanterelles on toast

About 1.5kg (3lbs) of clean chanterelles
Butter
Clove of garlic, crushed
A grating of nutmeg (optional)
Toast
Salt and pepper

METHOD

Cook the mushrooms slowly in a little butter in a frying pan. Add the garlic and cook until soft. Season well, adding a grating of nutmeg if you like it, and serve on buttered toast.

Cracked wheat with nuts and wild mushrooms

1 onion, finely chopped
30g (1oz) butter
300g (10½ oz) cracked wheat (bulgar)
700ml (1¼pt) vegetable stock
1 tbsp olive oil
450g (approx 1lb) mixed wild mushrooms, sliced
1 clove of garlic, chopped
50g (2oz) whole almonds
50g (2oz) whole hazelnuts
50g (2oz) sunflower seeds
Handful of lovage, finely chopped – if unavailable use parsley
Salt and pepper

METHOD

Melt the butter and fry the garlic and onion until soft and just starting to colour. Add the bulgar and stir for a couple of minutes, coating it in the butter.

Slowly add the stock, stir and bring to the boil. Cover and simmer for 12-15 minutes until the stock is absorbed. Take care not to overcook and let the bulgar go soft, you want to keep a little texture to it.

Roast the nuts and sunflower seeds in a dry frying pan until starting to colour. Allow to cool and then roughly chop the nuts. Slice the mushrooms so the pieces are roughly the same size, and fry gently in a little olive oil until soft and starting to turn golden. Gently combine everything, season and serve.

Jew's Ear Fungi

This may sound like something that requires a visit to a GP for some kosher ointment, but please read on as **Peter Litfoot** explains the merits of this rubbery fungi

Jew's Ear Fungus
(Auricularia auricula-judae)

Most people will know of some things that you can do with elderflowers and elderberries, but we are concentrating here on the decaying process of the old elder branches because they play host to a very interesting and common ear shaped edible fungus.

This fungus looks and feels like it should really not be edible, it's brown and rubbery and simply looks too ear-like to be appetizing. However, if you are prepared to try it, you may find you really do like it.

If that is the case then you are really in for a treat. Since elder trees are very common, so too is this fungus. It is sometimes found on other trees, but mostly you will come across it on a decaying elder branch. And, just like the elder, it's widely found all around Britain. Furthermore, since this is one of the very few frost tolerant edible fungi around, you can often harvest it in the depths of winter. It's also commonly available through the spring, and can, if you are lucky, be found all year around. Despite the look of them, they have a reassuringly pleasant mushroomy smell. Oh, and if you want to be politically correct, you can call it the Jelly Ear Fungus – see how versatile it is!

You should harvest these fungi when they are light brown in colour and rubbery to touch, once they are turning blackish and are hard they are past there sell by date. They are a little too rubbery to eat raw, and don't really have much of a flavour so they are often used in casseroles or soups. If stir frying or using within an omlette recipe they are most enjoyable when sliced thinly due to the rubbery texture. As with many wild mushrooms, it is a good idea to check that the creepy crawlies haven't already started eating them before you have, slicing helps here.

Drying

You can either dry the fungi cut into strips or dry it whole, they dry very well and can be reconstituted by soaking in water for around 15 minutes. Alternatively, once dried the fungi can be ground up for use in soups and casseroles.●

Picking

1 You want fresh fungi (see opposite), these are old ...

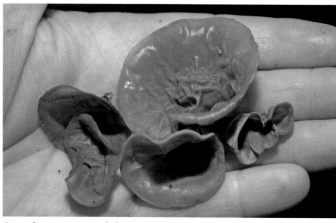

3 ... these are much better ...

2 ... and will not make good eating ...

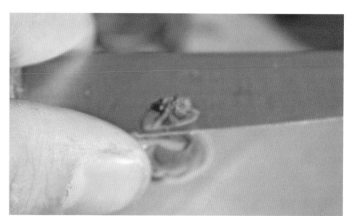

4 ... but remember to check for and remove any attached bark

Jelly Ear sauce

6 finely sliced Jew's Ears
Half an Onion, finely sliced
1 crushed clove of garlic
1 tsp finely chopped basil
50ml (1¾ floz) cream
Butter

METHOD

Melt the butter on a low heat and gently cook the sliced fungi for five to six minutes. Next add the onions and garlic and cook until they are translucent. Add the remaining ingredients, stir well and simmer gently for a further two minutes. This sauce goes well with a fish dish.

Jew's Ear soup

12-15 Jew's Ear Fungi
2 leeks
2 onions
1 large potato
25g (1oz) butter
500ml (1 pint) vegetable stock
200ml (7 floz) milk
2 tsp chopped chives
Pinch of salt & pepper

METHOD

Scrub and dice the potatoes and thinly chop the onions and leeks. Wash the fungi thoroughly several times and place in a pan with the butter (the fungi are more than 90% made up of water). Cover and simmer gently for 15 minutes. Add the vegetables and simmer for another 10 minutes. Add the stock, herbs and seasoning and cook for a further 25 minutes. Finally, stir in the milk, and serve. Alternatively, if you prefer, allow to cool, liquidize and re-heat before serving.

Jew's Ear and stilton omlette

This dish is so easy to make, it smells great while cooking and is delicious to eat. One of my favourites

About 4 good sized (4-5cm diameter) Jew's Ears
2 medium eggs
Splash of milk
3-4 chive stalks, chopped
Small sprig or margoram, chopped
50g (2oz) Stilton cheese
Black pepper

METHOD

Wash and slice the fungi and pan fry in a 50/50 mixture of olive oil and butter for a few minutes. Add some pepper for seasoning. Meanwhile prepare your eggs and milk, and mix in your finely chopped herbs. Remove the fungi from the pan and pour in the omlette mixture. Once the omlette is half cooked, after a few minutes, put the fungi back in, crumble in the Stilton and fold the omlette in half sealing in the fungi and the cheese.

Add the fungi and Stilton before folding the omlette

Sweet chestnuts

October is just about time to start collecting one of the most plentiful, useful, and tasty of all the free foods available. Sure, you can buy them in tins, or fresh in the shops when they're in season, but that's no fun, let's get harvesting!

Peter Litfoot gives advice and ten ideas for sweet chestnuts

The Sweet Chestnut tree (*Fagus castanea*) has been with us for thousands of years, having been introduced by the Romans. They are very easy to grow and can start to bear fruit within ten years.

Of course that's too long to wait, so if you don't have any cropping in your garden you will need to go out and about to find some. It's not at all difficult since they are very large trees growing to over 20 metres tall. In October they begin to drop their nuts profusely at the sides of roads, along country paths and in woodlands all over the country. They are easily got at by rolling the husks under your feet to open them up, which will reveal the leathery looking nuts inside. Be careful though not to prick yourself on the sharp husks. Be careful also not to come home with bucket-loads of conkers (horse chestnuts) they're not at all edible but appear at the same time of year. It's quite easy to tell them apart

since both the husks (the green casings) and the nuts themselves look different. The husks of the sweet chestnut are more prickly and the nuts are pointed at one end while conkers are not. As long as they are of a reasonable size, 80 chestnuts should come to about a kilo.

So long as you scrape away the sour second skin, fresh chestnut can be eaten raw and let's face it you've got to try a few while you're collecting them, haven't you? They can be eaten whole on their own or with other vegetables, and as a cooked ingredient they add a unique nutty flavour to many recipes, both savoury and sweet.

You can roast, boil or even microwave chestnuts with their skins on.

Roasting
It's important first to make a cut through the outer skin to prevent the chestnuts from exploding, then pop them onto a baking dish into a pre-heated oven at 190°C (375°F, Gas 5) for around

20 minutes. Turn them occasionally then remove from the oven, peel and enjoy! They are easier to peel while they are still hot or warm. Try also coating them with melted salted butter in a pan before roasting, you can then bake them in a hotter oven and they should be ready within around 10 minutes. You can also roast them over an open fire in a roasting pan if you have one!

Boiling
Again, make a cut through the outer skin and boil for five minutes, drain from the water a few at a time and peel. Sometimes they will simply pop out of the shell, but you may find it handy to use a sharp knife. As an alternative, to minimize flavour–loss with boiling, you could soak the nuts overnight in water without first cutting through the outer skin. With the skins softened they can then be boiled for 1 hour before peeling. Remember they are much easier to peel when hot so don't leave them to cool before peeling.

Microwave

Make a slit in the nuts, pop them onto a plate and cook on the roasting setting for two minutes.

So there are some easy ways to enjoy your harvest – fresh chestnuts can be stored in the fridge with your vegetables for up to six months. If you want to use them all year round (and don't want to buy them in the shops!) you can simply freeze cooked chestnuts once they are peeled and cooled in a freezer bag.

Cut through the skin before cooking

Boiling takes no longer than 5 minutes

Peel whilst still hot

Once cooked chestnuts can easily be frozen

Chestnut soup

A simple yet tasty soup to warm you up as the evenings get cooler!

Serves 4

500g (1lb) boiled or roasted chestnuts
One large onion, chopped
50g (2oz) butter
2 tsp sugar
Seasoning
1ltr (1¾ pints) vegetable stock

METHOD

Simmer the chestnuts, onion, butter and sugar in a pan with seasonings for 10 minutes. Add the vegetable stock and cook for a further 30 minutes. Allow to cool a little before liquidizing the soup, if preferred you can also pass through a sieve. Re-heat and serve with chunky brown bread.

Chestnut burgers

Serves 4

500g (1lb) cooked and mashed chestnuts
50g (2oz) plain flour
1 egg
½ tsp baking powder
Splash of milk
1 large onion, chopped and sautéed

METHOD

Mix all the ingredients thoroughly and with floured hands, make into burgers. Grill for 10 minutes on each side and serve straight away. Serve in buns with sauce or chutney and salad.

Burgers with a definite difference!

Chestnut, tuna and pasta salad

A surprisingly tasty variation to the quick and easy tuna and pasta salad

400g (14oz) wholewheat pasta (or any other if preferred)
200g (7oz) roasted or boiled chestnuts roughly quartered
280g (10oz) tuna chunks
Juice of a lemon
150g (5oz) mayonnaise
Pinch of pepper

METHOD
Boil the pasta for ten minutes, strain and leave to cool. Combine all the other ingredients thoroughly, then mix in with the pasta.

Chestnut, potato and Stilton bake

Preparation time 25 minutes, total cooking time 1 hour 10 minutes

Serves 4
500g (1lb) chestnuts, pre-boiled or roasted
500g (1lb) potatoes
2 large onions
1 tsp chopped marjoram
2 tsp chopped sage
250g (9oz) Stilton
Pinch of salt and pepper

METHOD
Scrub and chop the potatoes into small cubes and boil for 20 mins. Meanwhile sauté the onions until tender (about 10 minutes). Roughly chop or break up the sweet chestnuts. Crumble the Stilton. Strain the potatoes and, while saving some of the Stilton for a topping, mix all the ingredients thoroughly and place into a deep oven dish. Put on the Stilton topping and bake for 45 minutes.

Chestnut and apple stuffing

This is perfect to use as a stuffing inside a decent sized goose or turkey, or to serve on the side of a roast dinner with other vegetables. It can also form the basis of a meal in itself served with boiled or roast vegetables. It can be frozen and would make a great addition to a Christmas feast.

Cooking Time: 45 minutes
Total Time: 1 hour 20 minutes

1kg (2lbs) chestnuts, roasted or boiled, quartered
800g (1¾lbs) eating apples, cored and peeled and chopped into cubes
Half a day-old French loaf cut into small chunks
2 celery stalks, chopped
1 onion, diced
6 tbsp butter
400ml (¾ pint) vegetable or chicken stock
1 tsp salt

METHOD
Melt the butter in a large pan and cook the celery and onion for 10

minutes or until tender. Add the apples and herbs and cook for another couple of minutes, add the stock and salt and bring to the boil. Mix in the chestnut and bread thoroughly. Place into a glass baking dish, cover with foil and cook for 45 minutes in an oven pre-heated to 170°C (330°F, Gas 3). Alternatively use for stuffing anything up to a 7kg bird.

Beef and chestnut pie

A tasty, warming winter pie made with prime beef and chestnuts cooked in a rich, wine sauce, topped with a puff or shortcrust pastry lid. You can use cooked fresh chestnuts, tinned, frozen or vacuum packed for this recipe.

1 tbsp plain flour
Salt and pepper
1kg (2lb) braising steak, diced
3 tbsp oil
2 large onions, chopped
220ml (8 fl oz) red wine
3 despn tomato purée
200ml (8 fl oz) beef stock
2 bay leaves, crushed
450g (1lb) chestnuts, halved if large
275g (9-10oz) shortcrust or puff pastry
Beaten egg to glaze

METHOD

Add a sprinkling of salt and pepper to the flour. Toss the meat in the seasoned flour. Heat 2 tablespoons oil in a large pan and brown the diced steak in batches. Remove the meat from the pan. Add the remaining oil to the pan and cook the onions until they become transparent. Stir in the red wine, stock and tomato purée and add the meat and bay leaves. Bring to simmering point. Cook on a low heat for 1-1½ hours until the meat is tender. Add the chestnuts, adjusting the seasoning to taste. Transfer to a pie dish and leave to cool. Roll out the pastry and cover the dish, trimming off any excess and pinching the edges so that it adheres to the dish. Lightly brush with the beaten egg. Make a few small incisions in the pastry and cook for about 20-30 minutes gas mark 4/180°C/350°F until the pastry is crisp and golden brown and the filling is piping hot.

Chestnut and celery soup

1 litre (2 pints) of chicken/turkey stock
50g (2oz) butter
1 head of celery (the whole bunch)
250g (9oz) roasted or boiled chestnuts
1 onion finely diced
Sage leaves

METHOD

This simple soup relies on very good chicken stock. Remove the stringy bits from the celery with a peeler, and slice diagonally into 2cm (1 inch) diamonds. Melt the butter in a saucepan, add the onions, cook but do not brown. Add the celery and just cover with the stock. Cover saucepan with lid, and poach till the celery is tender, don't let the liquid boil! Add the chestnuts and a couple of sage leaves, and more stock. Allow to heat through, and serve with a fresh sage leaf.

Marrons glacés

These sticky chestnuts epitomise Christmas for me. Yes, they are time-consuming to make, and no, they don't look quite like bought ones but they are bound to be a hit.

1kg (2lbs) sweet chestnuts (as large as possible)
600ml (1pint) water

600g (1¼lbs) sugar
200ml (7oz) liquid glucose (available from pharmacies and some supermarkets)
2 tsp vanilla extract

METHOD

Preparation time three days, so don't leave this until the last minute!

Cut two or three shallow slits into the skin of the chestnuts and put into simmering water for half an hour. It's important not to let them boil, or they'll go hard. Remove from heat and allow to cool enough to handle. Remove the outer and inner skins. Don't worry if some of them fall apart a bit, keep the big chunks as you can still use them. Put the chestnuts onto a shallow baking tray, in a single layer (you may need to use more than one tray). Put the sugar and water into a pan and heat to 104°C using a sugar thermometer. Pour the syrup over the nuts and leave overnight to cool.

The next day, put the syrup back into the pan and heat to 110°C, pour over the nuts, as before, and leave overnight. Do this a final time the following day, but adding the glucose and vanilla to the syrup. Heat to 116°C this time and pour over the nuts. Transfer to a sterilised jar and seal, or allow to dry then wrap in foil or paper twists.

Chestnut and brandy cheesecake

This is more of a special occasion idea, great as an alternative Christmas dessert that you can make in advance – you can freeze it, or store it in the fridge for up to three days. It's actually surprising easy to make once you have gathered together all the ingredients. And WOW, you just cannot buy anything like this in the shops! Top tip – make two and freeze one – you'll be happier once you've eaten the first, knowing there's another one close on hand.

To serve 12 (one large or two small sized cheesecakes)

1kg (2lbs) ricotta cheese
500g (1lb) roasted chestnuts
4 eggs
200g (7oz) sugar
1 vanilla pod
150ml (¼pint) brandy
4 tbsp mixed peel
1 tbsp butter
Water

METHOD

Put the chestnuts, brandy and 100g sugar in a pan. Halve the vanilla pod, scrape out the seeds and add to the pan. Mix and cook on a high heat for 8 minutes. Be careful not to allow it to burn, add water (or more brandy!) if needed. Crush the chestnuts in the pan into small chunks and leave to cool. Meanwhile grease a 25-30cm diameter oven-proof dish for the cheesecake with the butter, and pre-heat the oven to 180°C (350°F, Gas 4). Mix the ricotta, eggs, remaining sugar and mixed peel in a bowl.

Gently blend the chestnut mixture into the bowl to achieve a marbled effect, try not to mix in too thoroughly. Bake in the oven for 1 hour then reduce the temperate to 170°C (330°F, Gas 3). Place the empty vanilla pods on the top of the cake for decoration and bake for a further 15 minutes. Remove the cake and allow it cool.

Serve while still warm with crème fraiche or vanilla ice cream, or alternatively serve chilled.

Chestnut and chocolate cake

This cake is made with chestnuts instead of flour and has a soft fudgy texture. It is suitable for people with wheat allergies. For those worried about sugar and fat, the quantity of both of these could be reduced as far as 55g without affecting the resulting taste too much.

4 large eggs, separated
250g (9oz) chestnut purée
110g (4oz) good quality dark chocolate
110g (4oz) butter or soft margarine
110g (4oz) caster sugar
A few drops vanilla extract

Line an 8 inch round cake tin with greaseproof paper or baking parchment. Set the oven to 170°C (330°F, Gas 4) to warm up. Break the chocolate into pieces and put it with the butter or margarine into a bowl fitted tightly over a saucepan of water that has reached boiling point. Reduce the water to the lowest temperature to avoid steam getting into the chocolate. Stir occasionally until melted. Do not let the hot water touch the bottom of the bowl or the chocolate will seize up and become unusable.

Meanwhile beat the egg whites in a mixer until stiff but not too dry. Reduce the speed of the mixer and beat in half the caster sugar. Fold in the remaining sugar and a few drops of vanilla extract with a metal spoon. The egg whites should look glossy and stand in peaks when the spoon is withdrawn.

Put the chestnut purée into the chocolate mixture, mix until smooth. Add the egg yolks and mix in well. Place a few tablespoons of the egg-white mixture into the chestnut and chocolate mixture and beat with the mixer to loosen the texture. Gently fold in the remaining egg white with a metal spoon until thoroughly incorporated.

Place the mixture in the cake tin and cook for about 1 hour (you may want to test at 45 minutes as some ovens or cake tins cook faster) or until the cake springs back when pressed gently and a skewer inserted into the centre of the cake comes out clean. Turn the cake onto a cooling rack. It can be eaten hot or cold. Dust with icing sugar and cocoa powder to serve on its own or with cream or ice cream.

Pheasants

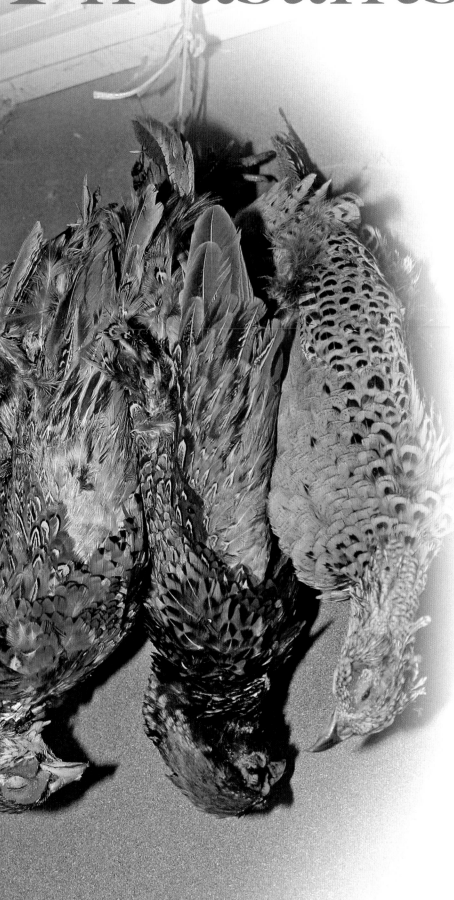

Every year hundreds of thousands of pheasants are reared for the UK shooting season which runs from October 1st to February 1st. This ensures a plentiful supply of this delicious bird, which is now readily available almost anywhere in the country. Only around 30% of these birds end up being shot, many of the rest are taken by foxes, stoats or other more exotic predators. Some do survive over the winter to rear their young, but without the intensive rearing for the shoots, pheasant would be a rare sight in the UK.

The birds are often sold in a pair, known as a brace – one male cock pheasant and one female hen pheasant. The hen is normally smaller than the cock and also, when it comes to eating, a little more tender.

Getting fresh birds

If you get the opportunity to shoot your own birds, or buy some birds fresh from a shoot, it is recommended that they are hung for at least a week, and up to three weeks in frosty conditions. Hanging helps to tenderise the meat and give it a good gamey flavour. If the skin is broken it may be best to hang the birds inside cloth or paper sacks to keep the flies off. I have converted an old fridge into a cold-store for hanging birds. This means I can hang them for a good three weeks and be sure that the flies can't get to them. If you want to do this, make sure the fridge still works and use it switched to minimum for hanging the birds. Remember to check regularly!

Plucking

Pheasants are not the easiest of birds to pluck by hand, but if you are just doing the odd one here and there, and are a little patient, it's not that much of a chore. It's best to start by pulling out the flight feathers individually or a few at a time, on the wings and tail and then work away at the back, coming round to the breast, then the legs and wings. Expect this to take up to around 15 minutes per bird if you are a beginner. Once completed you may like to marvel at the plucking rate for an experienced 'pheasant plucker' using a dry plucking machine – they can kick them out a rate of one every sixty seconds.

Gutting

To gut the birds, first chop off the head and neck, close to the body. Push a finger into the cavity and break away the wind pipe and the organs that are attached to the carcass. Next, with a sharp knife cut a slit around 4-5cm long above the vent (the anus). Draw out the intestines carefully, trying to keep them intact. If you are lucky you will draw out the organs (kidneys, liver etc) with the intestines. Reach in to ensure that everything is removed – the heart often needs pulling out separately. If necessary, clean the bird with a clean damp cloth prior to cooking or freezing, and if freezing we recommend you cook the bird within three months. ●

Pheasant recipes

Pheasant casserole

No feature on pheasant would be complete without the inclusion of a casserole. This is a relatively easy dish to prepare, and one that is almost impossible not to enjoy eating!

Serves 4

2 pheasants
100g (4oz) flour
1 tbsp oil
50g (2oz) butter
500g (1lb) mixed mushrooms
600ml (1 pint) stock
300ml (½ pint) red wine
1 bay leaf
½ tsp chopped thyme
Seasoning

METHOD

Joint the birds by halving and quartering them. Fry in the casserole pot with the mushrooms, oil and butter, turning until browned all over, about 5 minutes. Remove the pheasant pieces and mushrooms from the juices and set aside. Stir the flour into the juices and cook for a further 3 minutes before adding and stirring in the stock and then the wine. Add the herbs and bring back to the boil while stirring, then return the pheasant and mushrooms to the casserole pot and cook in the oven (preheated to 180ºC, 350ºF, Gas 4) for an hour. Remove the bay leaf and serve.

Roast pheasant with apples

Serves 4

2 pheasants
2 large cooking apples
50g (2oz) butter
Seasoning
1 tsp chopped thyme
100ml (3½ fl oz) port
2 tbsp double cream

METHOD

First bring the bird up to room temperature and ensure it is clean, if necessary wipe with a clean, damp cloth. Peel, core and slice the apples. Use half as a stuffing inside the birds, mixed with the thyme. Dot the birds with the butter and cover with the remaining apple slices. Cover loosely with foil and cook in a preheated oven at 210ºC (410ºF, Gas 6) for one hour, removing the foil 5 or 10 minutes before it is cooked

For the gravy, remove the apple stuffing and put in a pan with some of the juices from the bird or a little stock, then add the port and double cream and stir on a low heat for a few minutes. Serve with roast potatoes and fresh vegetables.

Roast pheasant basted with bacon

Most game birds are low in fat and benefit from heavy basting if roasted. Bacon and sausage meat are perfect for the job here

Serves 2

One pheasant
100g sausage meat
50-75g bacon rashers
2 tsp butter
One small onion
½ tsp chopped sage
½ tsp chopped thyme
Seasoning

METHOD

Chop the onion and mix with the sausage-meat and the sage and thyme. Use as a stuffing inside the bird. Season the skin with salt and pepper and cover with rashers of bacon and dot with the butter. Roast in a preheated oven at 210ºC for one hour. Remove from oven, rest for 20 minutes or so and serve with roast vegetables and gravy.

Roast pheasant with classic gravy

Lucy Young, author of *Secrets from a Country Kitchen* (Ebury Press) and *Aga Easy* (Absolute Press) shows us a great way to enjoy this popular game bird

Young birds can be roasted whole, giving good flavour and moist meat.

One pheasant for every two people
Salt and pepper
Streaky bacon
Parsley stalks
Lemon
Onion

For the gravy:
Plain flour
300ml (½ pint) pheasant stock
50ml (2fl oz) port or red wine
Worcestershire sauce
1 tbsp redcurrant jelly

METHOD

Prepare the pheasant(s), season all over and cover the breasts with streaky bacon. Fill the cavity of the pheasant with flavourings like parsley stalks, lemon slices and onion wedges.

Sit in a roasting tin, breast upwards. Roast in an oven pre-heated to 180°C (325°F, gas 4) for about an hour. Remove bacon and continue to roast for a further 10 minutes or until crispy brown and the pheasant is cooked. To test it's done, pierce the thickest part of the thigh with a skewer and when the juices run clear the pheasant is cooked.

To make the gravy, sprinkle a little flour into the fat in the tin to give a smooth roux. Whisk in the pheasant stock and port or red wine. Whisk until smooth, add a dash of Worcestershire sauce and the redcurrant jelly, bring to the boil, sieve and serve with the pheasant.

To cook in an Aga

Slide onto the second set of runners in the roasting oven and roast for about 40 minutes. Remove the bacon and continue to cook for a further 10 minutes, until the skin is crispy and golden brown. Test that the pheasant is cooked by inserting a skewer into the thickest part of the thigh; if the juices run clear the pheasant is cooked.

Rabbits

Rabbit is possibly the most common source of wild meat in Britain, and if you are able to regard this cute fluffy animal as food we will show you how to make the most of it.

Rabbits are very commonly shot and ferreted both as a sport and as a method of pest control. Given their habits of rapid breeding, digging holes on golf course, eating crops and young trees, landowners are normally very happy to have regular visits from the local ferret club for example. Some are also happy to pay to keep the population under control.

A day out ferreting would normally involve a small group of people with perhaps four or five ferrets and would likely end with a bag of 20 to 30 or more rabbits. This is certainly a more humane way of controlling rabbits than gassing or snaring. If you are interested in getting involved in ferreting, there are plenty of useful websites to look at such as www.britishferretclub.co.uk. If buying rabbits, you should be able to pick them up from 50p or even less to around £3 each.

While you can catch rabbits all year round, they are best in the months of September and October when they are well fed and neither breeding nor raising young. A young tender rabbit picked up at this time of year is likely to make a good plump specimen which can be ideal for recipes with shorter cooking times.

Gutting

The rabbit should be gutted as soon as is convenient. It's a quick, easy, clean and tidy procedure

With a sharp knife cut just the skin avoiding the membrane and guts, from the vent area up towards the head

Carefully cut through the membrane right up towards the head

This is what you should then see: a clean, tidy and complete packet of guts

The guts, if unbroken in this way are easily and neatly removed...

...leaving a clean cavity containing the heart, liver, kidneys and lungs.

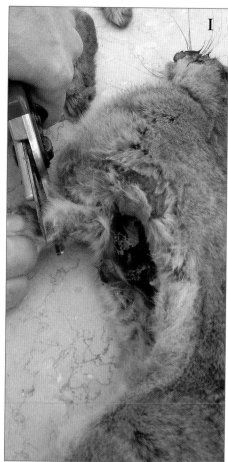

I

Cut or chop all the legs off above the knee joint with kitchen scissors or a good pruning shears

2

Cut the skin around the saddle (lower back) to separate the fur into two pieces

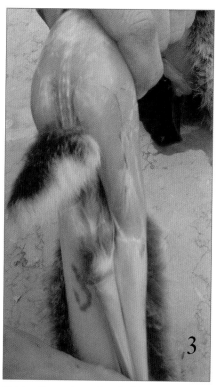

3

Take a firm grip and pull skin over and off back legs.

Skinning

To skin the rabbit you will need a strong pair of kitchen scissors or pruning shears that can easily cut though bones. Alternavtively you can use a meat cleaver and a chopping board.

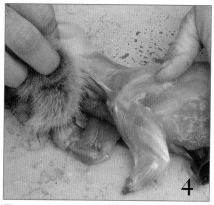

4

Then pull the rest of the skin either over the head or to the head which will then be chopped off

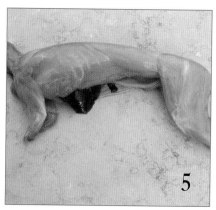

5

The carcass – now wasn't that surprisingly easy!

Jointing

Rabbits should not be hung, as so long as you have a fresh rabbit you should consider also making use of the heart, liver and kidneys.

The best way to enjoy eating rabbit is by cooking them long and slow to ensure that the meat is nice and tender. This makes rabbit ideal for casseroles.

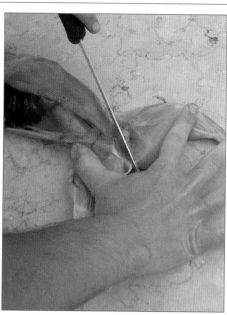

Removing the legs: cut where the muscles join the legs to the hips

Job done! Clockwise from top: back legs, front legs, heart, liver, kidneys, ribs, saddle and the thin flaps of meat that join the ribs to the belly

Put rabbit back on the menu

Rabbit may not be top of the menu for many of us but we're missing out on a tasty, healthy, organic meat, says **Paul Peacock**

Moonraker has absolutely nothing to do with James Bond. It is a title for a poacher, a rabbit poacher at that, who takes his bag and throws it into the village pond to avoid being caught with half a dozen bunnies. Then, at night, he would take his garden rake and get them out under the cover of darkness, raking the moon's reflection on the surface.

Our relationship with rabbits goes back at least a thousand years BC. 'Spain' is a translation of ancient Phoenician and means the 'land of the rabbit'. The Romans aided their spread to most of Europe as a food resource and the animal's movement around the world was completed by sailors, who set breeding colonies on every island they could find, for the same reason.

Rabbits are not rodents and have scrupulous habits of cleanliness. They live exclusively on green plants and will not forage among litter or pollution. Of course, they are cute and people keep them as pets, hence our squeamishness about eating, what has been for many centuries, the salvation of the nation's poor. Quite why rabbit stew is not our national dish, instead of bacon and eggs or a Sunday roast, is a mystery to me but there are many excellent reasons for eating them.

They are becoming a pest again in the countryside, and have almost recovered their numbers from the Myxomatosis of the 1950s. Secondly, they are such fantastic eating. The flavour is not gamey at all and, more importantly, it is healthy meat – low in fat, low in cholesterol, and high in protein. Thirdly, it is the most organic meat you can buy and all rabbit that has been taken from the wild has been dispatched completely humanely – no long journeys to the abattoir, no chemical pumped diets, no fear, no stress.

Another excellent, if political, reason for eating rabbit is to keep the control of its numbers away from the Government. Deliberately infecting them was a complete disgrace, and subsequent attempts to gas them were simply cruel because it was such an inefficient method; those on the periphery of the burrow were only half gassed and had long, painful deaths.

So, rabbit meat is possibly the best you can buy, even though it doesn't come in big steaks.

Buying rabbit

You may be able to buy rabbit from your local butcher, although I tried what seemed like every one in Manchester, without success – so you might need to order it, and they will skin and quarter the animal for you. If you get stuck you can buy online from http://www.woldsway.co.uk – a farm and meat processors. Some butchers sell rabbit off the bone, which allows for greater versatility and less waste. In France most rabbit is farmed and sold to exclusive Parisian restaurants. In the UK a lot of the rabbit is taken from the wild population by shooting or netting. But there is some farming, and some frozen meat is imported from abroad.

Cooking rabbit

Many recipes ask you to soak the rabbit in water before you start. This is a slight misunderstanding about the gameness of the meat – yes it is classed as game, but it is not strong flavoured like hare or pheasant. There is no real need to soak it at all, but you can marinade it to infuse subtle flavours.

Rabbit is low in fat, more so at the hindquarters than the shoulders, although even here it is much less fatty than chicken. It is therefore best cooked in a liquid to maintain its texture and not become dry. You can barbeque or grill rabbit, but frequently baste it or liberally brush with oil. For the same reason, microwaving rabbit is quite difficult and not really recommended. ●

The traditional way to hang a rabbit on a stick for collection. Rabbit game is not hung to improve flavour or texture, but should be eaten or frozen straight away

Notice how lean the meat is off the bone

The filling for rabbit pie

Adding a bouquet garni will give extra flavour

Rabbit recipes

Rabbit casserole in white wine

This should be our national dish!

Serves 4

50g (2oz) butter
1 onion, diced
75g (3oz) streaky bacon, rindless and chopped
2 cloves garlic, crushed
2 rabbits, jointed
300ml (½ pint) white wine
300ml (½ pint) chicken stock

METHOD
Fry the onions and garlic gently in the butter, until pale brown. Remove the fried onions and garlic and seal the rabbit joints in the remainder of the butter, to which a little oil has been added. Once the meat is seared, remove to an ovenproof dish and add the fried onions. (Some recipes call for the meat to be dusted with flour for this step). Add the wine and stock to the frying pan to incorporate all the fat and flavours and then pour this over the rabbit in the pot.

Cook in an oven, pre-heated to 160°C (325°F, gas 3) for an hour or until the meat is tender. Check for seasoning and if you wish, thicken the sauce with a roux.

Diana's jugged rabbit

Serves 6

3 rabbits, quartered
2 onions, sliced
3 rashers bacon, chopped
600ml (1pint) cider
Pinch of ground garlic clove
Herbs (bay, parsley, mint) in a bag
Salt and pepper
Flour

METHOD
Fry the bacon and onion in a little butter. Flour the rabbit pieces and fry in the juices until seared. Combine all the ingredients in an ovenproof dish and cook at 160°C (325°F, gas 3) for two hours, checking occasionally on seasoning and liquid level.

Beery bunny marinade

This uses a good light ale as a basis for a marinade for two rabbits.

For the marinade
500ml (17fl oz) Pale Ale
2 shallots, finely chopped
2 garlic cloves, crushed and chopped
Pinch of cayenne pepper
1 tbsp honey
2 rabbits quartered (or you can use 1kg/2lb diced rabbit meat)
Oil for frying

METHOD
Mix all the marinade ingredients and place into a sealable container, along with the rabbit meat. Keep in the fridge for 24 hours. Discard the marinade and fry the meat in a little oil until tender. Serve with salad, pitta bread and dips. You could skewer the meat with various vegetables and barbeque as an alternative.

Italian rabbit

Serves 4-6

Olive oil for frying
2 rabbits, quartered
2 cloves garlic, crushed
2 large onions, finely sliced
250ml (9fl oz) white wine
1 can of passata (small can, 500ml)
1 tsp thyme
2 bay leaves
1 tsp sweet basil, chopped

METHOD
Brown the garlic and onions in a large frying pan and add the rabbit to sear. Add wine to the onions and boil, then add the passata and herbs. Cook for 30 minutes on a simmering heat, check seasoning; serve with your favourite pasta.

Roast rabbit

Serves 4-6

2 rabbits
6-12 rashers bacon
Various cubed roasting vegetables –
potatoes, turnip, parsnip, carrot
Oil for roasting

METHOD
Rabbit needs to be kept moist when roasting. Place your peeled, cubed and washed vegetables in your roasting tin and sprinkle with salt. Cover with oil and cook for 30 minutes. Cover the rabbits with bacon to seal them during the roasting. Then add your two rabbits and baste with liquid from the tin. Cover with foil. Cook for a further 90 minutes at 180°C (350°F, gas 4) or until the meat is tender.

Rabbit pie

Serves 4-6

2 boned rabbits
1 onion, sliced finely
2 large carrots, sliced fairly thinly
1 tsp sage or thyme, whichever you prefer
Stock to just cover the pan bottom
Handful of peas, to add at end

For white sauce
25g (1oz) butter
25g (1 oz) flour
150ml (¼ pint) milk
Short crust pastry to cover

METHOD
Sauté the onion and carrot in a little oil and add rabbit to colour. Add stock to just cover the ingredients and herbs; cover with a lid and simmer for 30 minutes, checking if tender. Make a roux in a separate saucepan and gently add warm milk, stirring constantly to make a white sauce. Season as necessary. Add some of the simmering stock to dilute. Place ingredients in a pie dish, add the peas and pour the sauce mixture over the meat. Stir gently together to incorporate everything. Cover with short crust pastry and wash with beaten egg. Cook in an oven at 190°C (375°F, gas 5) for 30 minutes or until the pastry is cooked.

Rabbit duke
One of my favourite recipes and VERY easy to do!

Serve 4

Two rabbits, quartered
1 large onion, thinly sliced
2 tomatoes, sliced
50g (2oz) Cheddar cheese, grated
Salt and pepper

METHOD
Place the rabbit joints in a well-buttered dish. Slice an onion very thinly and place on top with two sliced tomatoes. Sprinkle on salt and pepper, then sprinkle grated cheese and a large knob of butter. Bake for about one hour in a moderate oven at 180°C (350°F, gas 4) or until tender.

You can serve rabbit duke individually with a single joint if you wish

Rabbit recipes

Rabbit casserole with wild rice and broccoli

Preparation time 30 minutes, cooking time 1 hour 15 minutes. Add mushrooms and bacon to the recipe for added flavour and to make a bigger meal.

Serves 4-6

1 young, fat rabbit, cut into six pieces
3½ tbsp olive oil
2 cloves of garlic, crushed
Bouquet garni (1 bay leaf, sprig of marjoram, parsley and thyme)
3 sprigs of rosemary
250g (9oz) small onions or shallots, sliced
150ml (¼pint) dry white wine
250ml (9fl oz) chicken stock
250g (9oz) mushrooms optional)
200g (7oz) chopped bacon optional)

METHOD

Best done in a cast iron pot or casserole dish, then you can serve it straight to the table. Lightly brown the rabbit portions in the olive oil on the hob. Remove rabbit and place in a sidepan and cover. Sauté onions (and bacon and mushrooms) until golden on a low heat (do not burn!). Return rabbit and season with salt and pepper, add the wine, reduce gently for five minutes, add the stock, herbs and garlic. Cover and cook on a low heat for 1 hour, do not let it dry out. Boil the mixed wild rice for 15 minutes and steam or boil the broccoli for five minutes. Remove the rabbit from the pot and serve with rice and broccoli.

Rabbit fricassée

Well, what can we say? When you try this (and the other recipes) you'll understand why rabbit is so popular with the French. This is a very easy to prepare meal, you just need to make sure you let it simmer gently then you can get on with other things while it cooks away! If you prefer you can serve the vegetables with the rabbit without puréeing them
Preparation time 12 minutes, cooking time 1 hour

Serves 4
1 young, fat rabbit
3 onions
3 carrots
3 parsnips
3 sticks of celery

2 potatoes
1 litre (1¾pints) of stock (vegetable or chicken)
Sprig of thyme
Sprig of rosemary
Clove of garlic
2 bay leaves
Seasoning

METHOD

Cut the rabbit into joints, place into a large saucepan or casserole dish, cover with stock and bring to the boil. Meanwhile, scrub and dice the vegetables and crush the garlic, chop up the thyme. Add all vegetables and herbs to the pot and stew gently for 45 minutes.

Remove the vegetables and liquidise to a purée with a little of the stock and re-heat. Place the rabbit joints onto plates and cover with purée, use the stock as a gravy.

Braised rabbit with mushrooms and cider

Serves 4

30g (1oz) butter
1 tbsp sunflower oil
4 Rabbit portions
4 small onions, quartered
375g (¾lb) mushrooms, quartered
300ml (½pint) dry cider
a few sprigs of parsley
3-4 sprigs of tarragon
Salt and black pepper
300ml (½pint) single cream
2 tbsp chopped parsley to garnish

METHOD

Melt the butter with the oil in a flameproof casserole. Add rabbit portions when the butter is foaming and cook for 5 minutes until browned all over. Lift out and drain on kitchen paper.

Add onions to the casserole and cook over a high heat, stirring for about 3 minutes, until golden. Add the mushrooms and cook, stirring occasionally, for 3-4 minutes until softened.

Return the rabbit to the casserole, add the cider, parsley sprigs and tarragon sprigs. Season with salt and pepper and bring to a boil. Cover and cook in a pre-heated oven at 160ºC (325ºF, gas 3) for 1½ hours or until the rabbit is tender.

Transfer the rabbit to a warmed dish and keep warm. Remove and discard the parsley and tarragon. Bring the sauce in the casserole to a boil on the hob, then boil until reduced by about a half. Stir in the cream, taste for seasoning and reheat slightly.

Pour the sauce over the rabbit and serve at once, garnished with a little chopped parsley.

Craddock's rabbit with hazelnut picada

I've dedicated this dish to some brave friends who've moved from London to an amazing 180 acres in Kent. There they grow hazelnuts (among other things) in glorious abundance, watched by an army of rabbits! When we visited them we left with bags and bags of hazelnuts, so with memories of sun-bathing rabbits fresh in our minds, this old gypsy recipe of Spain seemed very apt indeed.

We get our rabbits from a farmer on the Isle of Sheppey in Kent, they are of course wild, and they seem altogether nicer than the rather scrawny rabbits sometimes available from our local butcher. Picada just means minced or ground-up.

Serves 4-6

2 rabbits, jointed into smallish pieces (you should be able to get 7 or 8 pieces from each rabbit). Save the livers and kidneys and hearts from the rabbits
Olive oil, a lot
8 tomatoes finely chopped
2 onions finely chopped
2 cloves of garlic, crushed
Parsley, chopped, about a handful
Plain flour
250ml (8½floz) white wine
Salt and pepper
Thyme, fresh
Celery stick
Pinch of paprika

For the picada:
75g (3oz) toasted hazelnuts (don't worry if you can't find fresh ones, they are available from your local supermarket)
3 cloves of garlic, chopped
4 pinches of saffron
Olive oil
2 red chilli peppers, chopped
The cooked livers etc from the rabbits – cook them gently in a little olive oil beforehand.

METHOD
Make the picada by taking all the ingredients, putting them in a blender and whizzing till they are a smooth paste. Then put to one side while you prepare the dish.

Using a large frying pan (or a paella pan!), fry the onions in some olive oil till they are translucent and golden. Add the tomatoes, garlic and parsley, and simmer till the whole is reduced to a thick sauce. Then put it aside for the moment. Toss the rabbit pieces in a little flour, and using another pan and some more olive oil, fry them till they are golden on all sides, but not cooked through. Then add the rabbit to the tomato sauce you have just made, add the parsley, thyme, white wine and everything else, except the picada.

Gently cook everything for about half an hour, or until you think the rabbit is cooked through. Remove the rabbit and arrange on a suitable dish. Add the picada to the tomato sauce, adding some water if you need to thin the mixture, stir and continue to cook for a couple of minutes, then spoon over the rabbit, and sprinkle the smallest amount of paprika over the dish.

Serve with salad and potatoes mashed with olive oil.

Roadkill

This may not appeal to everyone, but what a pity it is that so many perfectly healthy and edible animals pointlessly die on our roads. *Peter Litfoot* says we should make more use of them.

The idea of eating roadkill may be just a step to far for some people, but it is something that many people do 'indulge' in, and something that deserves to be covered here. There are things you can and cannot do by law which we look at here, there are also some other important things to consider to ensure you enjoy the best the road has to offer.

The most popular meats on the 'roadkill menu' are probably deer, rabbit, pigeon and game birds. Interestingly, only last week I was talking to a local butcher who often gets called out by the police to shoot a distressed deer that has been mortally wounded in a road accident. Amongst other things, he makes the most delicious wild venison sausages.

The law

In the UK, to prevent people deliberately running over animals, the law states that you cannot take your own roadkill - you can take it as long as you have not killed it. There is some sense in this as the authorities do not want to be called out to rescue someone who had driven into a tree having made an overzealous attempt to run over a pheasant! However, nearly ten years ago, West Virginia, in the USA, passed a law making it possible for people to take home animals they have run over, partly in order to cut the costs of removing dead animals from the highways.

On our roads, you have to also consider the highway code. For example, anything seen at the side of motorways are clearly out of bounds since cars are only allowed to stop in emergencies or traffic jams.

Advice for beginners

The best way to ensure that anything you take from the roads is fresh is by sticking to a regular route on your daily travels. If you see something that wasn't there the night or morning before then it is probably pretty fresh, unless it has been dragged there by another animal, in which case it is likely to have been partly eaten. Clearly an animal will stay fresher for longer in a cool winter than a hot summer, and there will be less flies around too.

You need to check the animal over before taking it. Check that the intestines are intact, that the animal, if you pick it up. is a good weight. You need to be very careful if the intestines are broken, particularly with deer, as bacteria could contaminate the meat. Finally, make sure you have a suitable container with you.

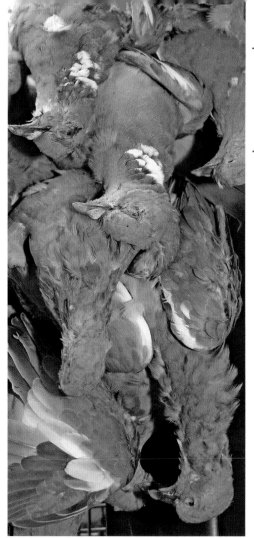

Pigeon

Pigeons do not associate the bang of the shotgun with death, and they will continue to land in the field in little groups of four or five birds. The weapon of choice is the 12 bore, either double barrelled or a repeating 12 bore with a single barrel. It is not uncommon to have a kill to cartridge ratio of 1 to 15; consequently there are many techniques to improve the chances of a kill, most of them associated with getting to know how pigeons fly and approach their food. As you get used to the trajectory of the birds you will anticipate what they are going to do next. You will have become a hunter, using your intelligence to catch and kill your prey.

Air-gun shooting

This is something of a challenge, the bird's feathers being quite a match for most air-gun pellets. You have to get close to the birds and aim for the head, which is the only hope you have for a clean kill. The most usual place for this sport is around a country farmhouse, where you can wait for the birds to arrive. You frequently need a pair of ladders to retrieve them. You will need a high powered air rifle with a good sight. Most of this shooting involves knocking them off a farm roof – be completely sure there is no chance of hitting anything beyond the birds.

Trapping

Pigeons can be trapped quite easily with drop traps or walk in traps. This is my least favourite method of getting pigeon meat, not because once trapped the bird has to be killed by hand, but because it is much more stressful for the animal. It is vitally important that you do not use this method unless you are exactly sure how to painlessly and efficiently kill a pigeon with your hands. It is much the same as killing a chicken, but not everyone can do it well.

A word of warning

Be sure your pigeons are completely disease free. Do not take them from towns or cities. Ensure you only take completely rural birds, those oily, railway-station, birds are riddled with all kinds of diseases.

They might not look it when they are wandering through Trafalgar Square and getting on Nelson's nerves, but pigeons are clever. Although its brain is inside a small head, it really knows how to use it. Because of this, pigeons are not easy to kill, but to many, this fact alone makes their eating all the better.

Shooting pigeons is not fun; it can be exhilarating, even addictive, but I believe strongly in the Old General's maxim: "If you're not prepared to eat it, you shouldn't try to kill it." The truth is that in rural areas, pigeons can eat their body's weight of crops in ten minutes. I personally believe it is better to shoot and eat the bird than poison it, or somehow kill it and simply waste the carcass.

Hide shooting

Usually set up in a line up to a mile long, shooters in hides, dressed in camouflage, wait for pigeons attracted to decoys both on the ground and set in flappers, which whirl lightweight plastic pigeons in manic circles. They arrive, downwind, from a copse or worse still, a corn field, and when still high in the air the birds side-wing, flying in a kinked zig-zag, which makes them almost impossible to shoot until they feel safe enough to slow down and begin their final approach, wings high and into the wind. This is the sportsman's chance, and the birds are shot when they feel safest.

This behaviour has evolved to give them every chance of escaping their wild predator, the peregrine falcon. Many a few dozen cartridges have been wasted trying to shoot a pigeon at the wrong time.

A shooting hide, tight in to a hedge, note how well camoflaged the shooter is too (pigeons have very good eyesight)

A half body, a DIY decoy made from a pop bottle a 'real' bird and a full body decoy

Mobile decoys - a battery powered flapper and a whurler

Pigeon behaviour

- *Pigeons like to land into the wind so set up your hide with this in mind*
- *They are attracted to movement, hence moving decoys are very successful*
- *Mobile decoys can attract birds from a quarter of a mile or more away*
- *The white flashes on the wings of the birds are a particularly strong attractant – bear this in mind with your decoys*
- *Pigeons only tend to land where food is available, be in the right place*
- *Pigeons thrive all year round by eating a wide variety of seasonal food*

Meat

Pigeons and shallots were made for each other. This is rich game that does not need hanging. The dark meat is very savoury, almost venison like, perhaps the tastiest meat you can get. It is also very healthy, but because it is so full of blood, there are pluses and minuses about it. On the plus side, there is a great sauce to be made from pigeon. On the minus side, it goes off ever so quickly. Do not leave unrefrigerated and use within a couple of days.

Those of you who do not fancy cleaning out a lot of pigeons should simply not bother. You can just take the breasts from the bird and discard the rest. Having taken this you have more or less 95% of the available meat .

Removing the breast meat is easy, as we show on the right. Alternatively, take 20 birds to your butchers and give him half in exchange for whatever dressing you like.

Remember the golden rule, if you are not prepared to eat, don't kill. Don't simply throw the carcass away – make stock from what remains. Finally, and there will be many who will tut and sigh at this, I always keep a bottle of antiseptic soap with me when I have been handling pigeons, or any animals in the wild, so that I can be sure of having clean hands when handling food.

Cleaning a pigeon is a difficult job because the guts are delicate and easily broken. Slice at the head and around the vent once you have pulled the skin off the bird, over the wings and legs. Trim these off with scissors. Carefully draw out the intestines, and reach inside for the liver and pluck (heart and lungs). The crop can be cut out from the neck.

The liver and heart can be used in the gravy, but the rest is discarded and the carcass washed to remove all congealed blood. A shot bird might well have intestinal remains inside the cavity, which should be cleaned.

Because of its small size, you can get the same problem with dryness as in much larger birds. I like to sprinkle the bottom of the pan with small pieces of butter and place on this a layer of chopped shallots, upon which the birds sit, probably one per person, three to a pan.

You can place herbs in the cavity and layer bacon over the breast, which should be uppermost. If you prefer, you can place a knob of butter under the bacon on each breast.

Cook for 45 minutes at 200°C (400°F, Gas 6). Once cooked, add a good glass of claret to the onions and allow to reduce to make the most wonderful sauce in the world.

Cutting out the breasts

Pluck the breast feathers 'against the grain'

No need to do any more than this

With sharp knife cut skin along breastbone

Pull away skin by hand

With sharp knife cut each breast out

The breast meat from just one bird

Skinning and drawing to make easy use of the carcass

Pull the skin off the bird over the legs, wings and head

Cut the feet, wings and head off with a strong pair of kitchen scissors

Cut across the vent and carefully draw out the intestines to avoid tearing them open

Opening up the chest cavity shows the (good sized) liver and heart are still in place

Tips for shotgun shooting

- *The bang from firing off a shot will send birds in the area up into the air, they may then be drawn in by your decoys*
- *When making your hide ensure you have easy access in and out*
- *If shooting in pairs, for safety take turns in shooting so that only one of you shoots at any one time*
- *Be aware of where your shot will land if it misses the target. Don't shoot in the direction of houses, ensure you know the area*
- *Put your hide up along a hedge, or tight into a large tree for natural cover*
- *Memorise where the birds are landing and pick them up half a dozen at a time*
- *Find a field that is the only food source in the area for the best chance of attracting more birds*
- *Sometimes the mid-afternoons can be a quiet time for shooting as the birds are more likely to be naturally feeding in the mornings up to mid-day, or later in the afternoon*
- *You can roost shoot an hour before dusk and use roosting decoys that you can put into the trees*
- *Ensure you have plenty of sacks for collecting the birds*

Did you know?

- *There is no closed season for pigeon, they can be shot all year round – that's why they are not classed as game*
- *The pigeon is the most prolific bird in the British Isles*
- *On average, if shooting with a shotgun you should expect to use 100 cartridges to kill 50 birds, some experienced shooters do a lot better though*
- *Shooting pigeons can be a bit like fishing for mackerel – sometimes you can get 10 birds in 10 minutes, sometimes none at all*
- *Most experienced pigeon shooters would consider 80-100 birds a good bag*
- *George Digweed holds the current world record for pigeons shot in one day - 661 birds!*
- *You can obtain a shotgun license from your local police station, it is a little like applying for a passport and last for 5 years. You will also need a lockable cabinet to keep it in.*
- *Experienced guides run pigeon shooting days and courses which cost from around £120*
- *When buying birds, expect to pay around £1.50 for a pigeon in feather or around £2 for an oven ready bird*
- *Pigeon shooters sometimes open up the crops of the first birds they shoot to give them an idea of what (and therefore where) the pigeons are currently eating.*

Aging the bird

Before you decide whether or not to de-breast your pigeons, and how you are going to cook them, it is useful to know whether you have old or young birds on your hands. Young pigeons are more tender and can be roasted whole, or the breasts cooked fast and served pink. Older birds are more suitable for pies and casseroles.

It is not easy to be sure of a pigeon's age unless you encounter the bird before it is plucked and drawn – which of course you will if you have killed it yourself. A flexible beak, a thick neck and a supple, pliable breastbone are all signs of a young bird. You may also perceive the 'flush of youth' in the fine colour of its feathers. If the bird is 'oven-ready', from a butcher or game dealer, you still have a bit to go on; try pressing gently to see if the breastbone is supple. Does the skin look slightly rosy, as if stretched from beneath by a plump and youthful breast? Or is it whitish grey, slightly wrinkled, contracting over a hard, prominent breastbone and tough, dark meat? Experience will sharpen your response to these factors, and in time you will be able to tell a youngster even through the clinging cellophane of its supermarket wrapping.

A good plump breast is a good sign

Check the beak for flexibility

You can buy a whole bird complete with feathers, oven ready (plucked and drawn) or individual breasts

Roast pigeon with blackcurrants

This recipe looks complicated, but it really is quite simple, the hardest thing is the shopping! There looks like quite a lot of ingredients in the stock, but these are essential to achieve a rich, full flavoured finished sauce. The stock also makes a great broth or winter soup.

Serves 4

4 pigeons
Vegetable oil
1 carrot, peeled and chopped finely
1 small onion, peeled and chopped finely
1 stick of celery, chopped finely
½ small leek, washed well and chopped finely
2 cloves of garlic, crushed
2 tbsp (30ml) red wine vinegar
1 glass of red wine
2 bay leaves
Sprig of rosemary
Sprig of thyme
5ml/1 tsp tomato purée
6 juniper berries, crushed
A few black peppercorns
Chicken stock
Touch of Cassis liqueur (optional)
55g (2oz) fresh blackcurrants
Salt and freshly milled black pepper

METHOD
Preheat the oven to 220°C (425°F, Gas 7). Remove the legs and carcasses from the pigeons to leave you with 'crowns', you can ask your butcher to do this for you. Chop up all the bones and legs, place them in an oven tray and roast until lightly browned.

Heat 2 tbsp of vegetable oil in a saucepan and add the chopped vegetables and garlic. Lightly brown over a medium heat, do not allow to burn.

Add the roasted bones to the vegetables, place in an empty oven tray over a low heat, add the vinegar and red wine and bring to the boil, scraping all the bits from the bottom of the tray, this gives the stock its flavour. When the bits have been loosened, add the remaining liquid.

Next add the herbs, tomato purée, juniper berries, peppercorns and stock. Bring to the boil and simmer for 30-40mins, skimming all the time.

Once cooked, strain well, put in a clean saucepan and reduce to a syrupy stock. Strain well again through a fine sieve.

To finish the sauce, reheat gently, add the Cassis (if using) and most of the blackcurrants. Do not boil the sauce otherwise the fruit will break up. Cover to keep warm.

Put the seasoned pigeon crowns, breast side down into an oiled ovenproof frying pan, keep turning to brown all over. Place in the oven to cook for 15mins. Remove from oven and leave to rest for five minutes.

Slice the pigeon from the crown, then carve each breast into three or four slices. Spoon over a little sauce and a few of the saved blackcurrants. This is delicious served with wilted spinach and cubed roasted potatoes.

Pigeon with green peas

This versatile recipe will work with any bird. The partridge is still shot in England in various places although it was been largely supplanted by the grouse. The type of shooting for grouse is called a driven shoot, where hundreds of birds are driven by beaters past the spot where stands a number of shooters. It was introduced by Prince Albert, and was almost the death of the traditional English rough shoot, where three or four men, with dogs, would work the countryside, the dogs setting the birds ready to be shot.

Serves 4

1 pigeon, duck leg, or poussin per person or 2 quails per person.
250g (8oz) smoked streaky bacon, chopped into small pieces
225g (9oz) small white onions or shallots, peeled
1tbsp flour
750g to 1 kilo (1½lb – 2lb) shelled fresh peas (fresh if possible)
Thyme, a few sprigs
Chicken stock (from a cube will do)
White wine
40g (1½oz) butter
Oil
Salt and pepper

METHOD

Put the birds into a pan with the butter and oil and brown them on all sides. Then put them into a suitable ovenproof dish. Garnish the birds with strips of bacon and sprigs of thyme. Put the bacon pieces and the onions into the pan with the butter and oil and sauté until they are golden. Then put them in with the quails. Spoon the flour into the original pan with the butter and oil, add the chicken stock, a cup, and a glass of white wine. Stir, then pour over the birds. Add the peas, and season with salt and pepper, and more thyme. Place in a pre-heated oven at about 200°C (400°F, Gas 6) for about half an hour if you're using quail, about 45 minutes if you're using pigeon, poussin, or duck legs. Remove from the oven when the birds are golden brown, remove any excess grease from the pan with a crust of bread. Serve by itself, there's no need for anything else.

Venison

You would normally need a license to shoot deer, so you may have to resort here to getting your meat from a gamekeeper or butcher!

Venison in beer

The meat just fell off the fork, the treacle and sugar make the sauce a little sweet

Serves 6

1 tbsp oil
25g (1oz) butter
1 head of celery, chopped
2 tbsp black treacle
50g (2oz) soft brown sugar
1.5kg (3lb) diced venison
600ml (1 pint) bitter beer
300ml (½ pint) beef stock
Seasoning

METHOD

Preheat the oven to 180°C (350°F, Gas 4). Brown the celery well in the oil and butter, seal the venison and place in casserole dish with the celery. In the same pan dissolve the treacle and sugar in the beer. Add stock and seasoning and bring to the boil. Pour over the meat and cover tightly and cook for at least 2 hours, adding more stock if necessary.

Braised venison in red wine

Serves 4

1kg (2lb) shoulder venison, sliced about ½ inch thick
25g (1oz) flour
3 onions, diced finely
400ml (¾ pint) red wine
1 bay leaf
1 clove garlic, peeled
6 black peppercorns, cracked
Seasoning
Pinch of sugar
Oil

The wine made the onions turn a lovely colour of purple while the flavour was very tasty.

METHOD

Heat oil in frying pan and brown venison. Transfer to braising dish and add remaining ingredients. Cover the dish and cook in oven 190°C (375°F, Gas 5) for 1½-2 hours.

Venison steaks with orange

Serves 6

6 venison steaks
150ml (¼ pint) Grand Marnier or other orange liqueur
50g (2oz) chopped shallots
50g (2oz) butter
50g (2oz) flour
450ml (¾ pint) stock
Pinch tarragon
Pinch chopped parsley
Seasoning
450ml (¾ pint) orange juice
25g (1oz) sugar

The steaks were lovely and tender while there was a subtle hint of orange. Gorgeous.

METHOD

Marinate the steaks overnight in the Grand Marnier. Cook the shallots in butter for one minute and remove from heat, add the flour and cook for a few minutes, stirring. Remove from heat, add the boiling stock, herbs and seasoning and bring slowly to the boil and cook for 3-4 minutes, stirring. Drain and season the steaks and saute for about four minutes on each side. Remove from pan and keep warm. Add the orange juice to the pan, then the sauce and bring to boil. Add the sugar to the sauce and pour over the steaks.

Venison offal - the vital organs

Like perhaps all offal, venison offal is seriously under-rated. Speak to your local butcher and you may be able to pick it up at a very reasonable price.

Ray Smith River Cottage HQ butcher about to tackle a complete set of venison offal. Ask your butcher which bits are which if you are not sure

Fried venison kidneys

This is a very quick, easy and tasty way to enjoy venison kidneys

Kidneys
2 tbsp buckwheat (or plain) flour
1 tsp seasoning (salt & pepper)
1 tbsp groundnut oil
1 tbsp butter

METHOD
Trim out the fat from the kidney (this may be easier if you halve it first) and slice thinly. Heat the oil and butter in a frying pan. Mix the seasoning and the flour and use to dip both sides of the sliced kidney before frying. Fry for no more than a few minutes on each side. Serve with a cooked breakfast, or as a light meal with salad.

Venison diaphragm

Yes even the diaphragm can be eaten, and it's really quite tasty too! Simply trim off any fat, slice thinly and cook as for the recipe for fried venison kidneys.

Removing the fat from the kidneys

Venison diaphragm, it really is as good as it looks!

Stuffed venison heart

Serves 2-4 depending on accompaniements

1 venison heart
For the stuffing
One onion, diced
4 slices of bread, toasted and crushed
Half a stick of celery, diced
50g (2oz) butter, melted
½ tsp thyme, chopped
1 bay leaf
Pinch of salt & pepper
Cooking oil or bacon rashers for basting

Cut the heart in half, wash away any blood clots from the ventricles. trim off any excess fat, remove vents and any sinews. Mix all the other ingredients, stuff the heart, putting the two halves together, baste with cooking oil, or rashers of bacon if you like. Wrap in foil and bake in a pre-heated oven at 200°C/400°F/gas 6 for one hour. If basting with bacon remove foil around 10 minutes before finished to brown.

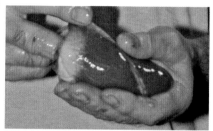

This heart was in very good shape, but they sometimes contain blood clots that need removing

Venison liver

The liver of venison should be a very good size and is ideal for pate making, is tasty sliced and fried with onions and garlic. However it is very important to start with a liver that is fresh and clean. If it is discoloured it should not be used. Clean the liver by soaking it in cold water for around an hour, changing the water two or three times.

Venison liver pate

If you like pate, you should try out this recipe which can be made in batches and frozen if needed.

450g (1lb) venison liver, finely chopped
2 medium onions, diced
2 cloves of garlic, grated
2 eggs, boiled
5 rashers of streaky bacon
1 tbsp groundnut oil
1 tsp salt
Pinch of pepper and 1 tsp crushed peppercorns

METHOD
Using a large pan cook the onions and garlic in the oil for about five minutes or a little longer, then add the liver and stir regularly until cooked, about another 10 minutes. Allow to cool and thoroughly mix in a blender with the remaining ingredients except for the crushed peppercorns and the bacon. Stir in the crushed peppercorns and transfer to a baking tin, cover with the bacon rashers and cook in a preheated oven at 180°C/350°F/gas 4 for 30 minutes. Remove, and leave to cool. Serve traditionally with crackers, bread or toast.

Ray demonstrating how to slice liver for frying

Dandelion and Burdock

This drink, so much nicer than almost anything else you buy in the shops, should be made in every house in the world. We should treasure our natural cordials because otherwise we might lose them altogether. There are communities in India that have now completely lost their traditional drinks; all they have are the ubiquitous soft drinks in cans and bottles that come out of the United States. These drinks had evolved over many hundreds of years, but are now gone forever.

Burdock is one of those plants we all know well. It nearly always grows near nettles, though it is not the same dock as the one you rub on nettle stings. The burdock has larger leaves and the flowers give fruits which are hooked or burred. You can take this plant at any time of the year, though young ones are best. The leaves used to be put on sprains and the seeds were crushed and drunk in tea to cure kidney stones.

The beer recipe below is an ancient one, and was a way of getting the very best use of the farmyard. Nettles, docks and dandelions grow best of all where animals have urinated. You can use this knowledge to tell where the animals in fields like to congregate. The nitrates which form in the soil are ideal minerals for growing many plants.

What is burdock?
(*Arctium lappa*)

The burdock has broad green leaves that can grow up to 18" (45 cm) long, considerably larger than the dock leaves often used as an antidote to nettle stings. The burdock can grow up to 2 metres tall but is usually much smaller than this.

It grows as a wild plant throughout the UK and Europe as well as many other places in the world.

If you thought that the dandelion had a pretty big tap root then you may be in for a surprise here. Burdock roots can be up to a metre long and two centimeters across.

The burdock bears prickly heads (burrs) which stick to animal fur in order to disperse the seeds very effectively. A study of these burrs led to the invention of Velcro by a Swiss engineer in 1948.

Extracts from the roots of burdocks are thought to have a range of medicinal qualities.

Burdocks should be easy to find in the wild, however, you may also be able to purchase them from garden centres which have a wide selection of herbs for sale.

Dandelion and burdock beer

This beer needs plenty of sweetness to work, and is best if supplied in the form of honey. The more honey you have, the better the drink. What you have to beware of is steeping the leaves too much. Some old recipes call for burdock leaves and root to be steeped for days. Those of you who have made comfrey tea in a pillowcase plunged into a barrel of water will realise that the smell is somewhat off-putting.

Ingredients
500g (1lb) Young nettle leaves
200g (7oz) Young dandelion leaves
200g (7oz) Burdock leaves
200g (7oz) Burdock roots shredded
1Kg (2lb) honey or sugar
2tbsp black treacle
Juice of 5 lemons
5 litres (9 pints) of water
Yeast

METHOD
Place the leaves and roots into the pan and add the water straight from the kettle and bring to the boil.

Simmer for 30 minutes and then sieve all the spent ingredients.

Pour the wort into a large sterilised fermentation bin and stir in the honey and the lemon juice.

When the liquid has cooled, but is still luke warm, sprinkle 1 tablespoon of brewers yeast and cover the vessel for a week.

Siphon the beer into sealable, sterile bottles, and add a spoonful of sugar to each bottle. This causes a secondary fermentation to add the extra fizz.

If you can, leave the bottles on a stone floor to allow the sediment to fall. If you simply put them onto floorboards, the vibrations in the house will not allow the spent yeast to settle.

After around a week or two you can start to drink the beer. It is not all that alcoholic, and in medieval times children would drink it along with adults.

Boil for 30 minutes.

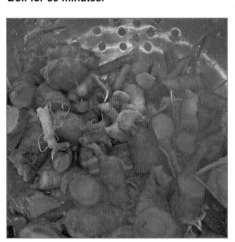

Strain off the ingredients and leave to cool.

Put into bottles, and drink after a week

Important

I never thought I'd ever have to write this. People these days have forgotten how to pour bottled beer. Perhaps your grandparents will remember the Mackeson adverts on the television. It showed an old chap carefully pouring his stout from a bottle, saying, "It looks good, it tastes good, and by golly, it does you good!"

Well, what he was doing was pouring the beer steadily, and once he had started, he couldn't stop. The whole bottle had to be poured out in one go without letting it fall back into the bottle at all. If he were to let it fall back, all the sediment would get mixed up and thus spoil the drink.

So when you pour real beer, like our Dandelion and Burdock, remember the sediment – it is not an ice cooled, mass produced larger drink you take directly from the bottle.

Dandelion coffee

W̲e have already written many acres' worth of information on the dandelion, *Taraxacun officinale*, whose scientific name means 'official cure for ailments.' Everyone knows the dandelion, but hardly anyone realises that it is botanically very similar to chicory, drinkers of French coffee will recognise as the bitter constituent. Camp coffee, those interestingly shaped jars of strong black liquid, used to be full of the herb.

It will be no surprise, then, that dandelion can be used as a coffee substitute. It is a little sad, actually, that we call it coffee at all. It aught to have a name all of its own.

1 Dig up the roots in the autumn when ground is soft to get long roots out intact and with the minimum of fuss. The roots will also be at their biggest

2 Cut off the leaves and discard unless some of the inner leaves are still good enough to be soaked overnight for use in salads

3 Wash and scrub the roots until they are quite clean

4 Cut the roots into 1cm long pieces, leave them to dry on a tea towel in a well ventilated place for ten days. Turn the roots once a day

5 Once dried, roast the pieces on a baking tray at 160°C (325°F, gas 3)

6 Either finely grate or grind the roasted roots in a coffee grinder, store in an air-tight jar and use a dessert spoon full of root per cup, allowing the root to infuse for about three minutes. Either use a strainer or make using a café-au-lait jar to filter out the pieces

7 You can drink as you would for normal coffee, although, due to a more bitter taste, you may enjoy it more with extra sugar or honey

8 You can also purchase dandelion coffee ready made from Herbs Hands Healing Ltd, £4.95 for 100g, 0845 345 37 27 www.herbshandshealing.co.uk

The Wild Food Year Book